ARTIFICIAL INTELLIGENCE

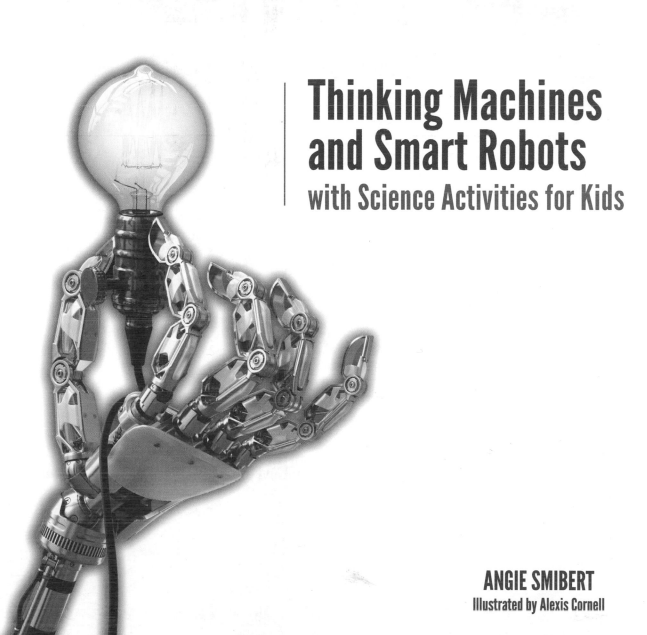

Thinking Machines and Smart Robots
with Science Activities for Kids

ANGIE SMIBERT
Illustrated by Alexis Cornell

Titles in the **Technology Today** book set

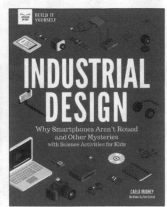
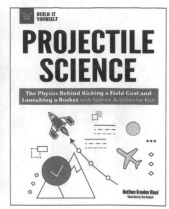

Check out more titles at www.nomadpress.net

Nomad Press
A division of Nomad Communications
10 9 8 7 6 5 4 3 2 1

This book was manufactured by Friesens Book Division
Altona, MB, Canada
August 2018, Job #244130

ISBN Softcover: 978-1-61930-675-2
ISBN Hardcover: 978-1-61930-673-8

Educational Consultant, Marla Conn

Questions regarding the ordering of this book should be addressed to
Nomad Press
2456 Christian St.
White River Junction, VT 05001
www.nomadpress.net

Printed in Canada.

Contents

Timeline . . . iv

Introduction
What Is Artificial Intelligence? . . . 1

Chapter 1
The Hunt for HAL: Early Forms of AI . . . 10

Chapter 2
Good Morning, Alexa: AI Today . . . 26

Chapter 3
AI in the Future . . . 41

Chapter 4
Do We Need AI? . . . 63

Chapter 5
AI in Science Fiction . . . 78

Chapter 6
The Debate Around AI . . . 97

Glossary | Metric Conversions
Resources | Essential Questions | Index

Interested in Primary Sources?

Look for this icon. Use a smartphone or tablet app to scan the QR code and explore more! Photos are also primary sources because a photograph takes a picture at the moment something happens.

If the QR code doesn't work, there's a list of URLs on the Resources page. Or, try searching the internet with the Keyword Prompts to find other helpful sources.

🔎 artificial intelligence

1942: Isaac Asimov publishes his three laws of robotics.

1950: Alan Turing creates the Turing test to determine if a machine is intelligent or not.

1956: The term "artificial intelligence" is coined at a Dartmouth College summer conference.

1958: John McCarthy invents LISP to program early AIs.

1966: Joseph Weizenbaum introduces ELIZA, an early natural language processing program.

1968: The movie *2001: A Space Odyssey* is released.

1973: "AI winter" begins, a time when interest in, and funding for, research on artificial intelligence is low.

1977: The AI characters C-3PO and R2-D2 appear in *Star Wars*.

1981: The first commercial expert system is introduced at Digital Equipment Corp. AI winter ends.

1997: Deep Blue beats world chess champion Garry Kasparov.

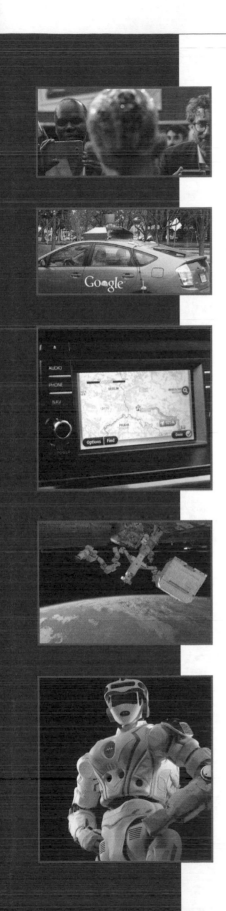

2002: The Roomba robotic vacuum cleaner is introduced.

2004: The DARPA Grand Challenge, a contest for autonomous vehicles, takes place for the first time.

2011: An AI named Watson wins the game *Jeopardy!*

2011: The development of Siri is announced.

2012: The first DARPA Robotics Challenge takes place.

2014: Alexa is introduced.

2014: Chatbot Eugene Goostman claims to have passed the Turing test, but, in reality, does not.

2016: AlphaGo beats world Go champion Lee Sedol.

2017: The Space Robotics Challenge takes place.

2018: A self-driving car hits and kills a person for the first time, causing people to question whether autonomous cars are a wise idea.

science fiction
sentient
autonomous
bionic
programmer
social intelligence
Industrial Revolution
Internet of Things
humanoid
matrix
strong AI
GPS
algorithm
AI assistant
sensor
DARPA
logical
robotics
artificial intelligence
expert systems
big data
cue
data
biotechnology
weak AI
digital
Go
fuzzy logic
profiling
machine learning
Turing test
gear
singularity
neural network
android
simulate
chatbot
glitch
lidar
axon
processing power
doomsday
dictation
dwarf planet
prototype

WHAT IS ARTIFICIAL INTELLIGENCE?

Can computers think? Can they learn? Will machines ever match humans in the ability to think critically and creatively? **Artificial intelligence (AI)** used to exist only in **science fiction** books and movies. Today, we have cars that can drive themselves, robots that can walk on their own, and computer programs that can answer our questions and find solutions to different problems.

What exactly is artificial intelligence? AI means different things to different people, and our understanding of it has changed through the years. Artificial, of course, refers to something made by humans, such as a machine. Intelligence is trickier to define.

ESSENTIAL QUESTION

Is there a difference between acting intelligent and being intelligent?

WORDS TO KNOW

artificial intelligence (AI): the intelligence of a computer, program, or machine.

science fiction: a story about contact with other worlds and imaginary science and technology.

human intelligence: the capacity for logic, abstract thought, understanding, self-awareness, communication, learning, emotional knowledge, memory, planning, creativity, and problem-solving.

grandmaster: a chess player of the highest class who has won tournaments.

supercomputer: a powerful computer.

forfeit: to surrender a game.

Scientists don't even really agree on what intelligence is in humans. **Human intelligence** differs from animal intelligence, and it might differ from computer intelligence, too.

One way to define human intelligence is to include the following abilities.

- To learn from experience
- To reason and solve problems
- To remember information
- To cope with life

In the early days of AI, scientists started with a basic definition. AI is a computer or machine behavior that would be judged intelligent if it was something a human did—such as winning a chess match.

DID YOU KNOW?

A chess match is when players play more than one game to see who wins the most.

By that definition, a computer named Deep Blue might be considered intelligent, since it beat **Grandmaster** Garry Kasparov at chess. If a human did that, we'd consider them intelligent. However, Deep Blue beat Kasparov by calculating hundreds of millions of moves per second. Is this the same as human intelligence?

The computer didn't truly understand what it was doing, not like a human would.

Scientists have been working for decades to develop computers that can think. It wasn't until close to the end of the last century, though, that they made a significant breakthrough with Deep Blue, an IBM **supercomputer**.

Garry Kasparov playing chess with young Tunisian players
credit: Khaled Abdelmoumen

HUMAN VS. MACHINE

Billed as the chess match of the century, the 1997 match between Garry Kasparov and Deep Blue featured human vs. artificial intelligence. In the second game of the match, Kasparov, the human, set the trap. He baited his opponent to take his pawn. Deep Blue, the IBM supercomputer, didn't fall for it. Instead, the AI made a masterful, human-like move. Kasparov was stunned.

Several moves later, the grandmaster rubbed his face and sighed. Deep Blue would beat him in six moves. Kasparov **forfeited** the game and walked off the stage. The AI had won.

WORDS TO KNOW

glitch: a minor malfunction.

logical: in a way that is orderly and makes sense.

sacrifice: to give something up for the sake of something else.

advantage: something helpful.

processing power: the ability of a computer system to accomplish work.

This game changed everything— both for the match and, it seemed, for AI research.

Kasparov had won the first game of the match, but he didn't win another. Deep Blue won the second, and they tied the next three games. In the sixth game, Deep Blue beat the human player in 19 moves.

Deep Blue won the match.

It was the first time a computer beat a human champion in a traditional chess match. Arguably one of the best players ever, Kasparov had never lost a match to either a human or computer.

Kasparov had even beaten Deep Blue a year earlier. In 1996, during the very first game Deep Blue and Kasparov played against each other, the human didn't win easily. Deep Blue made a move that didn't seem **logical**—it **sacrificed** a pawn. This move didn't have an immediate **advantage**, but chess players plan many moves ahead. A human player might have done this. Kasparov himself might have done this, but he didn't think a computer could "think" like that.

Kasparov was wrong! During the year between the two matches, IBM had time to improve Deep Blue into a machine that could beat the best player ever in the ultimate problem-solving exercise of chess.

Rematch!

Some experts think Kasparov might have actually tied Deep Blue if he hadn't withdrawn from that second game in 1997. Others think a computer **glitch** made the computer pick a random move, which then threw the human player off his game. Kasparov even thought for a while that IBM cheated. Why was it hard for people to believe a computer could beat a person at chess?

You can watch a news report on the chess match at this website.

PS

Kasparov Deep Blue video

The press, the public, and AI researchers hailed this as a great breakthrough. But did this victory mean that Deep Blue was intelligent?

Did it mean the machine could think like a human?

Researchers still aren't sure of the answers to these questions. Deep Blue wasn't really thinking like a human. It could look at the chess board and calculate 200 million possible moves a second. Up until 1997, supercomputers didn't have the computing power to do this for many, many moves ahead. Deep Blue was the first that could do this. In just one second, Deep Blue could see it might get that pawn back in six moves or that it would lose if it took Kasparov's bait.

Deep Blue had the memory and **processing power** and speed to consider billions of possible moves. Then, it could pick the one with the best chance of winning. Does the ability to do a massive number of calculations in a second make a computer or robot intelligent? That depends on how one defines AI.

strong AI: machine intelligence that follows the same patterns as human learning.

weak AI: machine intelligence that is focused on one task.

machine learning: a type of AI where a computer can automatically learn and improve from experience without being programmed.

algorithm: a set of steps that are followed to solve a mathematical problem or to complete a computer process.

Go: a game played between two players who alternately place black and white stones on a board to try to surround more territory than the other player.

robotics: the science of designing, building, controlling, and operating robots.

speech recognition: the ability of a computer to identify human speech and respond to it.

natural language processing: the ability of a computer to understand human spoken and written language.

diagnose: to determine the identity and cause of a disease.

humanoid: looking like a human being in some ways.

Many AI scientists think that for a computer to be considered intelligent, the way it does a task is just as important as its ability to do that task. For instance, what if the computer learned to play chess the same way a human player does? The computer might watch people play and then practice until it mastered the game. Would that make the computer intelligent? It might. Or it might not! Researchers don't agree—and they've split into two camps: **strong AI** and **weak AI**.

STRONG AI VS. WEAK AI

Strong AI researchers believe that a computer must do something the same way a human would to be considered intelligent. These researchers see the goal of AI as building computers that possess well-rounded, human-like intelligence.

In weak AI, sometimes called narrow AI, researchers think of AI as any system that exhibits intelligent behavior. How it exhibits this behavior doesn't really matter. These scientists see the goal of AI as solving problems. Weak AI tends to be **machine learning** focused on doing one kind of task. Weak AI might also simply be an intelligent **algorithm**, which is a set of rules a computer follows to solve a problem.

Many recent breakthroughs in AI combine these approaches. For example, an AI may "learn" how to identify faces on social media, but that's all that particular AI does. Another example is a new supercomputer called AlphaGo, which learns how to play the game **Go** by watching and playing millions of games.

Areas of AI Research

Today, AI research focuses on several areas. Each of these areas goes into making a computer or robot move, see, hear, and speak like a human. Do you think AI needs to feel human-like to be useful? Here are some of the things scientists consider when exploring new AI designs.

> **Robotics**

> Computer vision

> **Speech recognition**

> **Natural language processing**

Artificial intelligence is everywhere, yet, in many cases, we don't even realize it! Supercomputers still play games and win increasingly complex games such as Go and *Jeopardy!* We ask a personal assistant such as Alexa or Siri to tell us a joke, send emails, or turn off the lights. Self-driving cars can be found in much of the world. Robots are learning to walk, use tools, and climb over rubble. Social robots interact with humans.

Behind the scenes, AI identifies and even bans certain photos on social media. AI sorts through medical data and helps doctors make **diagnoses**. AI even writes bad poetry or screenplays. Yet, we're still far from a true thinking machine similar to those in our imaginations.

In this book, you'll learn more about how computers interact with the world and what they can do to improve our lives. We'll also think about the future of AI and imagine what human-computer relationships will look like in 50 years. Along the way, you'll do lots of hands-on activities and even invent your own AI!

Pepper is a **humanoid** robot able to read human emotions. It is used in stores and offices to send messages, sound notifications, and chat with visitors.

credit: Tokumeigakarinoaoshima (CC BY 1.0)

Engineering Design Process

Every engineer keeps a notebook to keep track of their ideas and their steps in the engineering design process. As you read through this book and do the activities, keep track of your observations, **data**, and designs in an engineering design worksheet, like the one shown here. When doing an activity, remember that there is no right answer or right way to approach a project. Be creative and have fun!

Problem: What problem are we trying to solve?
Research: Has anything been invented to help solve the problem? What can we learn?
Question: Are there any special requirements for the device? An example of this is a car that must go a certain distance in a certain amount of time.
Brainstorm: Draw lots of designs for your device and list the materials you are using!
Prototype: Build the design you drew during brainstorming.
Test: Test your **prototype** and record your observations.
Evaluate: Analyze your test results. Do you need to make adjustments? Do you need to try a different prototype?

Each chapter of this book begins with an essential question to help guide your exploration of AI. Keep the question in your mind as you read the chapter. At the end of each chapter, use your engineering notebook to record your thoughts and answers.

ESSENTIAL QUESTION

Is there a difference between acting intelligent and being intelligent?

TAKE A TURING TEST

In 1950, an English computer scientist named Alan Turing (1912–1954) devised a test to tell a person from a computer. You're going to try this with a chatbot. This is an online computer program that is designed to mimic a human.

❯ **Write down five questions** you think a computer might find hard to answer.

❯ **Pick one person to be the interrogator and ask the questions.** This person should not be able to see the computer or the human. They can be in another room or behind a curtain.

❯ **A second person will be the human answering the questions.** A third person will be the computer who will type the questions to the chatbot and then write out the answers.

❯ **With an adult's permission, the person playing the computer** should go on the internet and visit cleverbot.com. Here, you can type to an AI.

❯ **Have the interrogator ask the questions.** Rather than answering out loud, the "human" and the "computer" should both write down the answers.

✱ Can the interrogator figure out which is the human answering the questions and which is the chatbot? Why?

Try This!

Try thinking up a new list of questions that reveals which subject is the computer. Do you need to ask more specific questions? Questions about feelings and ideas? What kind of language does the computer use that makes you realize it's a computer?

Chapter 1

THE HUNT FOR HAL:
EARLY AI

Today, many of us have Siri on cell phones and Alexa in the kitchen to answer questions. AI algorithms predict movies we might like to see or music we might want to hear. Some people even have a smart home, where everything can be controlled with AI, from opening the door to turning on the heat.

Of course, it wasn't always like this. Ask an adult if they had AI when they were a kid! Even 10 years ago, AI was most often found in science and technology labs. And 60 years ago, engineers were just beginning to think of the possibilities for **programming** computers for different uses, including in business, war, **academics**, and everyday life.

ESSENTIAL QUESTION

How did the definition of AI change during the twentieth century?

However, many hundreds of years ago, people were already wondering what might happen if objects had the ability to interact with humans and learn new things. The ancient Greeks, Romans, and Chinese were curious about how things might be improved.

BEFORE COMPUTERS

Though computers and robots are relatively new, we've been building calculating machines and **automatons** for centuries. Automatons are machines that move like people or animals. The ancient Greeks built water-powered machines and other complex devices. One inventor even built an owl that moved and whistled.

Watch scientists talk about and demonstrate the Antikythera mechanism!

PS

Antikythera mechanism project overview

DID YOU KNOW?

In 1770, Hungarian inventor Wolfgang von Kempelen (1734–1804) built an automaton to play chess. He called it the Mechanical Turk. It caused a sensation in Europe because the automaton seemed to make intelligent moves. However, the Mechanical Turk was soon exposed as a fake. A human chess master hid inside the machine!

While we know about most of these ancient devices through writings, one mysterious machine has survived. In 1902, the Antikythera mechanism, as it came to be called, was discovered in a shipwreck off the coast of the Greek island of Antikythera. More than 2,000 years old, the small device puzzled researchers for years.

Finally, in the twenty-first century, scientists were able to scan it with a powerful new 3-D X-ray. The X-ray revealed the interior of the mechanism.

WORDS TO KNOW

solar system: the collection of eight planets, moons, and other celestial bodies that orbit the sun.

gear: a rotating part with teeth.

interest: the fee charged or paid for the use of money.

programmer: a person who writes computer programs. Also called a coder.

Researchers could then recreate the mechanism. They now understand that the device is a complex mechanical computer that tracks the cycles of the **solar system**. Its mechanism, as with most early machines, ran on a system of clockwork **gears**.

DID YOU KNOW?

The first robot, Unimate, was invented in 1950. Unimate was an industrial robot arm. First installed in a GM factory in 1961, Unimate's job was to stack hot pieces of metal.

In the 1700s, automatons became very popular among European inventors. They built figures, like puppets, that moved on their own by way of a clockwork mechanism. The automaton was usually built to do one thing, such as write a letter, play a song, or draw.

THE FIRST COMPUTERS

Charles Babbage (1791–1871) was an English mathematician who designed the first automated computing engines in the 1820s. But he never actually built them!

Babbage wanted to make calculations more reliable. In the 1820s, people who worked as engineers, builders, and bankers relied on printed tables of numbers to do their calculations. For instance, a banker would use tables of **interest** calculations to figure out how much money a customer had earned.

Difference Engine No. 2

The first Difference Engine was not actually built until 2002! Engineers constructed it faithfully from Babbage's plans. It consists of 8,000 parts, weighs 5 tons, and measures 11 feet long!

PS Watch the Difference Engine in action.

🔍 computer history Babbage engine

Babbage discovered that many of these books of tables had errors. So, he decided to design a machine to do the calculations instead. He drew up some plans for a new device. In 1833, he even built a small section of it. He held parties to demonstrate what he called his Difference Engine.

Ada Lovelace (1815–1852) met Babbage at one of these parties, and they became acquaintances. Ten years later, she translated a French article about the engine, and, more importantly, she added her own step-by-step notes on how to use the engine to solve problems. With those notes, Ada Lovelace became the first **programmer**!

Alan Turing

Alan Turing was a British mathematician and a pioneer in computer science. In the 1930s, Turing invented the Universal Turing Machine, which can be considered a model of a computer. During World War II, he led the British codebreakers at Bletchley Park, many of whom were female, to crack Germany's secret Enigma code. Enigma was a machine the Germans used to encode messages during the war. Turing, along with fellow codebreaker Gordon Welchman (1906–1985), invented a machine to help break the code. After the war, Turing continued his work on the Turing machine, which led to the Automatic Computing Engine (ACE). This was an early version of the modern computer.

Turing was prosecuted in 1952 for homosexual acts, which were illegal in Britain then. He died two years later. In 2013, Turing was granted a pardon.

The Turing machine, reconstructed by Mike Davey, at Go Ask ALICE at Harvard University
credit: Rocky Acosta (CC BY 3.0)

WORDS TO KNOW

morphogenesis: the development of patterns and shapes in living organisms.

Turing test: a test for intelligence in a computer.

The first working computers were not built until the early 1940s. At the time, the world was at war. In 1941, German engineer Konrad Zuse (1910–1995) built the Z3 computer. He used it for calculations related to airplane wing design. The computer was destroyed in a bombing raid in 1943 during World War II.

On the other side of the battlefield, British codebreakers built a series of computers called Colossus between 1943 and 1945. Colossus is considered the first programmable electronic computer. It helped break the German code called the Lorenz Cipher.

TURING AND THE THINKING MACHINE

In 1950, computer scientist Alan Turing asked an important question that led to the field of AI that we are familiar with today. Can a machine think? If so, Turing wondered, how could one tell a thinking machine from a human?

DID YOU KNOW?

While at school, Alan Turing was interested in **morphogenesis**, or the development of patterns and shapes in biological organisms. He thought these patterns were caused by chemicals spreading and reacting with each other across space. His work on this is still considered relevant.

This question gives us insight into what it means to be intelligent. To answer his own questions, Turing came up with a test. In the **Turing test**, one person asks both a computer and another person questions. The interrogator is separated from the computer and other person by a screen.

If the computer can fool a person into thinking it is human, the computer is considered intelligent. The computer must have knowledge and reasoning skills and speak natural language in order to mimic a human being. It's a huge task and, so far, no computer has passed the Turing test.

Turing realized that it was an enormous task to build a fully intelligent computer capable of passing his test. Plus, in the 1950s, the technology didn't exist yet.

Turing proposed the idea of a child machine. This was a machine that would grow into an "adult" thinking machine. Turing also proposed the idea of using the game of chess to test computer intelligence. Since chess is a logic challenge, mastering chess was a sign that the program was intelligent, at least in a narrow way.

Unfortunately, Turing died in 1954 at a young age, before he could do more work on creating and testing machine intelligence. Even though the term "artificial intelligence" didn't exist for a couple more years, he's considered by many to be the founder of AI.

A PHRASE IS BORN

The term "artificial intelligence" was first used at Dartmouth College in the summer of 1956. A computer scientist named John McCarthy (1927–2011) coined the term when he sent invitations to other researchers to come to Dartmouth for a conference on AI.

McCarthy, along with fellow researchers Marvin Minsky (1927–2016) of Harvard University and Nathaniel Rochester (1919–2001) of IBM, proposed that scientists work together that summer. They studied how machines might use language, form concepts, solve problems, and learn.

A statue of Alan Turing at Bletchley Park, made from about half a million pieces of slate quarried in Wales.

credit: Dirk Haun (CC BY 2.0)

During the conference, McCarthy even designed the first AI programming language, called LISP. This language was used to program many early AIs.

COMPUTERS PLAYING GAMES AND CHATTING

Through the 1950s and 1960s, researchers focused on getting computers to solve math and logic problems and to "talk." These activities were considered intelligent. Other activities, such as walking, were not.

Those early AI researchers who focused on problem-solving turned to games. The ability to learn and play a game was considered intelligent. Why do you think this is?

Computer scientists programmed computers to play different games, such as checkers, tic-tac-toe, and chess. Researchers at Oxford University, for example, wrote a computer program that played chess and checkers. At first, the program was slow.

In 1959, IBM computer pioneer Arthur Samuel (1901–1990) wrote a checkers program that let a computer play itself to learn the game. This was the first self-learning program, which Samuel called machine learning. The computer went on to beat the Connecticut state checkers champion.

Other researchers focused on getting computers to understand and respond to natural language. Computers were able to understand only machine or programming language.

Fuzzy Logic

Fuzzy logic is a type of AI algorithm. In the 1980s, fuzzy logic was used in controls for devices such as cameras and anti-lock brakes. Here's how it works! Traditional logic treats everything as either true or false, off or on. Fuzzy logic lets more advanced AI think in terms of degrees. For instance, with traditional logic, a car's brake is either off or on when the driver presses the brake pedal. It doesn't matter how hard he or she mashes the pedal down. With fuzzy logic, though, the brake can be 30 percent on if the driver puts their foot down very lightly. This gives AI control over the degree to which something happens!

WORDS TO KNOW

pattern matching: checking whether information follows a pattern.

expert systems: computer software that mimics the reasoning of a human specialist.

mortgage: a legal agreement where a person borrows money to buy property and pays it back with interest during a number of years.

Natural language is what people speak or type. In 1966, computer scientist Joseph Weizenbaum (1923–2008) of the Massachusetts Institute of Technology (MIT) wrote ELIZA, a computer program that could answer questions with reasonable responses. ELIZA used something called **pattern matching** to come up with the answers.

In pattern matching, researchers create a database of words or phrases along with the appropriate replies. The computer program checks a sequence of words or numbers for an exact match. Then it offers a reply that goes with that pattern. For instance, ELIZA had a program called Doctor.

Using this program, a person might say they're feeling sad. ELIZA's program recognizes the phrase, searches its database for the match, and then answers, "Did you come to me today because you're feeling sad?" That sounds like a reasonable response! However, ELIZA's pattern matching is simple by today's standards.

AI WINTER

Throughout the 1950 and 1960s, researchers and the public were excited by dreams of thinking machines. But by the 1970s, AI had not lived up to the hype.

DID YOU KNOW?

When ELIZA was first tested on people, many of them thought she was a real person and grew attached to her. Researchers were surprised at the strong emotions many users felt for their new doctor! The phrase "Eliza effect" now refers to the tendency of people to assume the words of a computer are those of a human.

Funding for AI research began to dry up. Many researchers realized just how far they were from creating real AI. The period from the early 1970s to the mid 1980s came to be called AI winter. High-profile work on AI stopped.

Not all work stopped, though. During the AI winter, researchers took different approaches to AI. Many continued to work toward strong AI in their search to create a true thinking machine able to do lots of different jobs. But some researchers shifted to a bottom-up, weak AI approach. They were interested in creating programs that worked on specific problems.

This weak AI sowed the seed for the comeback of AI in the 1980s.

ELIZA

In the 1960s, ELIZA was programmed as a "counselor" program that responded to people's mental health concerns.

You can still try it out at this website. Can you figure out the patterns ELIZA uses to answer questions?

PS

🔍 try ELIZA

AI SPRING

By the mid-1980s, AI began to flourish again. This time, researchers focused more on solving specific problems than building a computer with a full range of capabilities. AI returned in areas such as **expert systems**. Researchers tried to capture human expertise and feed it into computer systems to create knowledge bases.

For instance, a bank might have used an expert system for **mortgage** lending. The system contained everything human bankers had learned about home loans.

WORDS TO KNOW

neural network: a computer system modeled on the human brain.

digital: characterized by electronic and computerized technology.

neuron: a cell that carries messages between the brain and other parts of the body.

This knowledge could be used by different people working at the bank, which made finding answers to questions much more efficient for the bankers and the customers.

AI returned in other ways that people didn't even notice, too. AI could be found in the new fuzzy logic controls in autofocus cameras and in anti-lock brakes, for instance. When you aim your camera and the camera focuses on your friend's face automatically, that happens because of AI! Later, in the 1990s, AI would lend itself to other challenges, such as how to search the internet for information.

MACHINE LEARNING AND NEURAL NETS

In the 1990s, big breakthroughs in AI happened in two related areas—machine learning and **neural networks**. Both have their roots in the 1950s.

Remember Alan Turing? Back in the mid-twentieth century, Turing dreamed of a child thinking machine that could learn. And a few years later, Arthur Samuel taught a computer to play checkers, another example of machine learning. Samuel even coined the term "machine learning." But significant progress wasn't made in this area until 40 years later.

Machine learning is the process of computers learning—or teaching themselves—tasks.

DID YOU KNOW?

An experience called the AI effect occurs when something that is AI becomes such a standard part of our experience that we no longer think of it as AI. For example, speech recognition was once considered an essential part of AI. Today, it seems rather commonplace—and not really AI.

In the 1990s, computer scientists decided that instead of feeding computers human knowledge and telling them how to organize it, they would simply give the computer vast amounts of data and let the computers learn to make decisions about this information. Scientists created programs that would analyze data and draw conclusions from the results. The machines learned.

The internet made this machine learning possible. With the invention of the World Wide Web in 1989, the internet boomed. As it grew, more and more **digital** data was being stored online. AI researchers realized they could teach computers to learn and then plug them into all that data.

Machine learning is really a series of algorithms that give the computer the ability to learn. An algorithm looks at the data and then makes predictions and decisions based on that information. Have you ever wondered how websites such as Netflix and Amazon figure out what movies to suggest for you?

A machine-learning algorithm might sort through your previous movie choices, notice that you like science fiction movies, and recommend a new science fiction movie to you.

How does it do this? By using a neural network. An artificial neural network is a computer program inspired by how scientists believe the human brain works.

In the brain, **neurons** connect and send signals to each other. A neural net mimics this behavior. Artificial neurons are organized into levels, often called layers. The lower layers take in the information and analyze it. Then, they pass it to higher, hidden layers. These layers process the data further and then pass it to output layers.

This is where the computer makes a prediction or decision based on the output.

WORDS TO KNOW

deep learning: learning by studying examples and representations instead of memorizing facts.

Let's imagine that the neural net is shown millions of pictures of dogs of all shapes, sizes, and colors. Using this information, the net learns to recognize the pattern of a dog. When a new picture pops up, the neural net can tell whether it's a dog or not. The AI has taught itself to recognize dogs!

Researchers are not sure if this is how our brains work, but the method works for AI.

In the 2000s, recent advances in computer power have made something called **deep learning** possible. In deep learning, the neural net can have many, many more hidden layers. Much more information can be used and learned from.

In the short history of AI in the twentieth century, we've gone from the thinking machine being a fictional idea to AI being a part of everyday life. Often, we're so used to AI that we don't even recognize it! However, we haven't gotten the fully intelligent computer or robot we've dreamed about in movies, television, and books. In fact, our idea of AI has changed and adapted to include things that the early AI pioneers never expected.

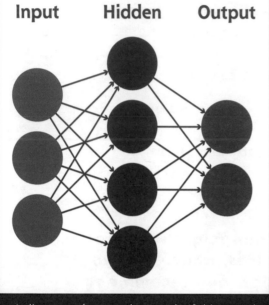

A diagram of a neural network. If this neural network were suggesting movies, the input layer would be movies you've already seen, the hidden layer would be where the computer processes this information, and the output layer would be the movies the computer thinks you might like to see.

Input   Hidden   Output

ESSENTIAL QUESTION

How did the definition of AI change during the twentieth century?

EXPLORE SCRATCH!
MAKE A MAZE GAME

Scratch is a visual programming language where the code is made up of graphic pieces that fit together like a jigsaw puzzle. Scratch was developed by computer scientists at MIT to help people learn to code.

❯ **With an adult's permission, go to** the Scratch website. Explore the site and check out programming examples.

❯ **Click "Tips" on the site and do the "Getting Started" tutorial.** Explore some of the other tutorials, too.

❯ **Now try the Maze Starter project** by searching "Maze starter" in the search bar. It's a project to learn how Scratch works and how to build with it.

❯ **Play the game!** Click the green flag to make it run. Notice what happens when the ball hits a wall or passes over the finish line.

❯ **Next, click "See Inside" to study how the game was made.** Click each of the sprites to see the code that makes each sprite act. If you click the ball sprite, you'll see the bits of code that make the ball move.

❯ **Now it's your turn.** Click "Remix." You can make changes to the code and the sprites and save your changes as your own project. You can make the maze more complicated, change characters, and add sound. Share the project with others on Scratch!

Try This!

Try out some other visual coding languages and apps, such as Hopscotch and Tynker. How do they compare to Scratch?

CODE ON PAPER

One of the first games AI researchers programmed a computer to play was tic-tac-toe. Have you ever played? It's a game with simple rules and strategies. Think about how you might program a computer to play tic-tac-toe. How would you explain it to someone who doesn't know how to play? How would you break down those instructions into simple moves? You're going to write a program on paper that a person can follow.

Remember, a program—also called code—is just a set of instructions to follow!

❯ **In your engineering notebook, define the problem.** What is your goal? What does the code need to do?

❯ **Do some research on the game.** What are the rules of tic-tac-toe? (You probably already know this!) What are some strategies for playing? Play a game against yourself or a friend. Take notes on moves you make. What else do you notice? For example, do games always end in a tie? Are there squares that are better to start with than others?

OXO

In 1952, British computer scientist Alexander Douglas (1921–2010) developed the first video game. It was a tic-tac-toe game called OXO, or Noughts & Crosses. The game let one human play against the computer. Douglas wrote the program on EDSAC (Electronic Delay Storage Automatic Calculator), one of the first stored-program computers. That is, EDSAC kept the code for the game in its memory. EDSAC was programmed to play a perfect game.

❯ **Write some code!** Write instructions for one player, X or O, since you'll be playing the other. Write out step-by-step instructions for winning a game. Computer code is often written in if-then statements. For example, if you were writing code for a maze game, you might write instructions such as this.

✱ "Go forward one space. If player hits a wall, turn left. If not, go forward one space."

✱ For tic-tac-toe, you might use steps such as this: "Put an X in the corner. If there's already an O there, then go to the opposite corner."

In 1978, two students built a computer out of Tinkertoys. This computer can play tic-tac-toe! **You can see photos of it at the Computer History Museum.**

🔍 **(PS)** 🔍 computer history Tinkertoy

❯ **Test your code.** One player will be the human and the other will be the AI following the code. For example, the human player will put an X somewhere on the grid. The AI player should look at the instructions to see what to do. If you get stuck, take notes. What do you need to change to make your code work?

❯ **Revise your code!** You may have to test your code and revise it a few times. This is what real programmers do.

❯ **Play one last time.** Write down your observations. Did it turn out as you expected? Did the game end in a tie, for instance? Do you think the paper program is intelligent? Why or why not?

Try This!

Try writing an algorithm for another simple game, such as rock, paper, scissors!

Chapter 2

GOOD MORNING, ALEXA:
AI TODAY

Alexa, play some music! Siri, how do I get to the coffee shop? Many of us already talk to AI in our living rooms, on our phones, and in our cars.

Alexa, Google Assistant, and Siri are voice-controlled **AI assistants**. They can play us music, read us books, answer questions, play games, help us navigate, and even control smart devices such as our televisions and lights. We can do this, for the most part, by making requests with just our voices—and most of the time, the AI understand us.

But these assistants are not even the most impressive AIs in our lives today! The early twenty-first century has been a breakthrough time for artificial intelligence. AIs such as AlphaGo and Watson are not only winning harder and harder games, they are also changing areas such as medicine and policing. AI is all around us, even in places we don't expect.

ESSENTIAL QUESTION

How has AI exploded in the twenty-first century?

SPEECH RECOGNITION AND NATURAL LANGUAGE PROCESSING

How did scientists create programs such as Alexa and Siri? Speech processing has been a very difficult problem to solve in AI research. Humans learn to recognize and understand speech at a very early age. We can separate voices from background noise. We understand that some words have many different meanings. We can figure out different accents. We know if a speaker means "their" or "there."

Humans also understand that meaning can change with **pitch**, **tone**, or volume—that means we can tell the difference between a question and statement. All of this is very hard to teach an AI. Computers understand the written word much more easily.

AI researchers had limited success cracking this problem in the 1970s and 1980s. Some breakthroughs were made in the 1990s. For example, a company called Dragon Systems introduced software that converted words people spoke to words written on a screen. But this early **dictation** software was slow and not very accurate.

Watch a short video about communication between humans and computers.

science talking computers

In the 2000s, though, AI researchers applied machine-learning techniques to speech recognition. AIs learned to recognize words and meanings by listening to millions of words, commands, and sentences. Machine learning led to voice-savvy AI assistants, including Siri, Alexa, and Google Assistant.

WORDS TO KNOW

patent: a document from the government that gives an inventor the exclusive right to make, use, or sell his or her invention.

Internet of Things (IoT): the interconnection via the internet of computing devices embedded in everyday objects, enabling them to send and receive data.

simulate: to imitate certain conditions for the purpose of testing or study.

sensor: a device that measures and records physical properties.

AI ASSISTANTS

AI assistants are relatively new. Apple released its assistant, Siri, for iPhones in 2011. Google developed Google Now in 2012 and Google Assistant in 2016. As of 2017, Alexa from Amazon has gained a large share of the voice AI market. She came on the scene in 2012. That's when four Amazon engineers filed a **patent** for a voice-based AI device that eventually became Alexa, the voice of devices such as the Echo and Echo Dot. The first Echo was introduced in 2014.

Alexa and the other voice-based assistants are examples of machine learning in action. Alexa learns from her mistakes on the job. Every Alexa collects data from her customers, and Amazon uses that data to continually improve the voice-based assistant.

Have you ever talked to Alexa? How do you address her differently from your family and friends? People use different phrases when they command Alexa to do something. To get music to stop, they may tell her, "Stop!" or "Quit" or "Cancel." They might even say, "Wait, I meant Beyoncé!" or "No, don't play that!"

Alexa learns from this input and gets smarter the more she's used.

An Amazon Echo device
credit: Crosa (CC BY 2.0)

However, Alexa, Siri, and Google cannot carry on real conversations. When you ask one of them what their favorite music is or their opinion on a book or movie, they won't give you a real answer because they don't have real opinions. Yet.

"Alexa, try this!"

You can try out Alexa online at this website. You will need an Amazon account to use it. The Alexa Skill Testing Tool is a **simulation** of Alexa that software developers can use to test new skills, such as playing Jeopardy! or controlling a smart device.

PS Ask Alexa to tell you a joke—or why the sky is blue.

🔎 try Alexa

DID YOU KNOW? By 2020, it's expected that the **Internet of Things (IoT)** may include 26 billion devices!

Voice assistants can also interact with smart devices such as lights, fitness trackers, cameras, thermostats, and even cars. These devices and other things with **sensors** make up what is called the Internet of Things (IoT). As this web of devices grows, voice assistants will be able to connect and control more and more things. Can you think of ways this will make your life easier?

ALPHAGO

In October 2015, AlphaGo beat Fan Hui (1981–), the European Go champion. AlphaGo is an AI designed by DeepMind, a company that is now part of Google.

The 2015 match between AlphaGo and Hui was the first time a computer beat a professional Go player.

The next year, the AI beat Lee Sedol (1983–), a world champion with 18 titles. Many consider Sedol to be one of the best Go players in the world for the past 10 years. During the game, AlphaGo played several inventive moves, even one that challenged hundreds of years of Go wisdom. In March 2016, AlphaGo earned the highest professional ranking, another first for a computer!

Ready, Set, Go!

Go is an ancient strategy game invented in China more than 2,500 years ago! The rules are simple. Two players take turns laying down black and white stones on a board. If the stone of one color is surrounded by the other color, the stone is taken prisoner. The player who captures the most prisoners and territory on the board wins. Though it sounds simple, Go is much more complicated than chess. In chess, there are 20 possible opening moves. On a Go board, the first player has 361 possible moves!

The newest version of the Go-playing AI, called AlphaGo Zero, learned to play the game just by playing against itself!

AlphaGo has a deep neural network. It learned to play by watching thousands of **amateur** and professional Go matches. Then, the AI played millions of games against itself. With every game, it learned from its mistakes and got better. This is called **reinforcement learning**.

AI BEHIND THE SCENES

Powerful AIs are not just for games. Many deep-learning AIs are already at work solving problems behind the scenes, in places that involve a lot of data. Some AIs, including IBM's Watson and those from DeepMind, are working on problems in medicine.

For example, at an eye hospital in Texas, Google's AI is reading eye scans. It trained by reading scans from hundreds of patients with various stages of eye disease. The AI is learning to spot eye disease at its very earliest stages.

The match where Lee Sedol was defeated by AlphaGo took place in Seoul, South Korea, on March 15, 2016. **You can watch the final moments at this website.**

PS

AlphaGo beats Lee Sedol

Why have a computer perform a task that doctors train for years to be able to do? Doctors at this hospital are flooded with patients. All of these people need eye scans before being diagnosed. The AI can speed up this process and leave doctors free to see more patients.

Likewise, DeepMind is working with the United Kingdom's National Health Service to develop more AI tools that can help improve health and wellness for people. An AI at Stanford University is learning to spot breast cancer cells in **biopsies**. And IBM's Watson is learning to diagnose diseases, recommend treatments, and perform other medical tasks.

WORDS TO KNOW

streamline: to make a process simpler and more effective.

predictive: able to accurately guess an outcome.

big data: extremely large sets of data that can be analyzed to reveal patterns and trends.

Medicine isn't the only area where AI is hard at work. It's being used to spot online hackers who are trying to find and steal personal information. It's also being used to **streamline** legal research, target customers, recommend stocks, and even prevent crime—to name just a few jobs.

It's Elementary, My Dear Watson

In 2004, an IBM engineer was watching American Ken Jennings (1974–) have the longest winning streak ever on *Jeopardy!*, the popular game show. The game gave the engineer an idea. *Jeopardy!* would be the next challenge for IBM's supercomputer, Deep Blue, which had already conquered the game of chess in the late 1990s. Seven years later, IBM's AI, now called Watson, beat Ken Jennings and another champion on television. To win, Watson drew upon a database of 200 million pages of facts, including all of Wikipedia. In 2014, IBM started programming Watson for a wide range of applications, including medicine.

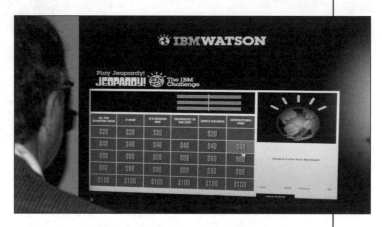

IBM employees testing Watson

credit: Raysonho @ Open Grid Scheduler / Grid (CC BY 3.0)

 You can watch Watson beat *Jeopardy!* champions at this website.

🔎 Watson Jeopardy!

Police in many countries are already using PredPol, a **predictive** policing AI. PredPol learns a city or town's crime patterns from historical data and then gives police daily lists of potential crime hotspots to check out.

The early twenty-first century is an exciting time for AI. Researchers have cracked key problems, such as natural language processing, as well as complex games. We can now talk to AI assistants, which gives us a hint of what it will be like to have voice control of smart devices.

Researchers have also learned from games. They've applied those algorithms to tackling **big data**, which is what researchers call the huge amount of information that exists on the internet.

Eh?

Researchers at MIT trained their deep-learning neural net, called SoundNet, to recognize sounds. They presented the AI with clips that contained a variety of sounds, including background noise. SoundNet learned to pick up individual sounds and predict the scene. You can try some of the training clips!

The video is blurred so that you can make your own guesses as to what the sounds are, while seeing the AI's predictions.

PS

ρ SoundNet MIT

This will bring big changes to the future of medicine, policing, law, and other professions.

In the next chapter, we'll look at what some of these developments mean for the world in the future. Self-cooking kitchens? Crime-fighting robots? What do you want to see?

ESSENTIAL QUESTION

How has AI exploded in the twenty-first century?

BUILD A MODEL OF A NEURON

Neural networks are modeled after human brain cells, called neurons. The neuron takes in information through its dendrites, processes the information, and then passes on the information to the next neuron through its axons. Let's make a model of a neuron.

❯ **Do some research. What do neurons look like?** With an adult's permission, search online and at the library for information about neurons. Find some photos of real neurons. Make sure they're from humans or at least mammals! Medical school sites can be good sources of information.

❯ **Using the images you find as guides, make a model of a neuron.** Label the different parts. From your research, can you explain what each part does? How does information travel in a neuron?

❯ **Once you've made one neuron,** add a few more to create a network.

Try This!

Take a photo of your neural network and share it. In a caption or tag, describe how information flows through your network!

WORDS TO KNOW

dendrite: a short, branched extension of a nerve cell that receives impulses from other cells.

axon: the long, threadlike part of a nerve cell that sends signals from the cell body to other cells.

NEURONS FIRING!

The neurons in your brain use both electrical and chemical signals to communicate. They pass information from one neuron to the next. Neural nets do the same thing, only with numbers! Let's build a very simplified model of how the information might flow from neurons in an eye to the brain.

❯ **Cut a straw into several small pieces.** You'll need only three pieces now, but you might want more later if you expand your network. These pieces will be the signals that the neuron sends when it fires!

❯ **Draw a large y-shape on a piece of cardboard.** Then place pushpins at the end of each line and where they intersect. Label the two pins at the top of the Y as A. These represent neurons in the eyes. Label the pin in the middle B and the last one C. Cut pieces of string long enough to join each part of this mini-network. Thread a section of straw onto each piece of string.

❯ **Tie strings around each pushpin and tighten** so that the straw slides easily between the pins. Push the first two straw pieces toward A, and the third one toward B. Now you have a mini-network of neurons!

❯ **But when do they fire? Let's set some rules.** The A neurons fire off a signal only when the eye sees an even number on the dice. The B neuron fires when it gets more than one signal. Then, when the C neuron gets one signal, it tells the brain, "Hey, we see something even!"

❯ **Roll some dice!** If one die has an even number, slide the signal straw from A to B. If both are even, fire off both signals. If the B neuron got two signals, fire off another signal!

Try This!

Make your mini-network more complicated! Add more strings, A and B neuron pins, and signals. All should lead to C (for now). You can even try changing the rules for when the neurons fire. How does that affect the information flow?

PERCEPTRON

In 1957, Frank Rosenblatt (1928–1971) of Cornell University invented the simplest neural net possible—the perceptron. It has inputs, a hidden layer, and an output. The perceptron is modeled on a neuron. The perceptron works the same way as a neuron—only mathematically.

The perceptron takes in numbers (X), adds them up in the hidden layer (also called the processor), applies a function, and spits out a number (Y). The function can be a question such as, "Is this a negative number?" or "Is this over a certain value?" While these are useful things to know, the answers don't indicate intelligence.

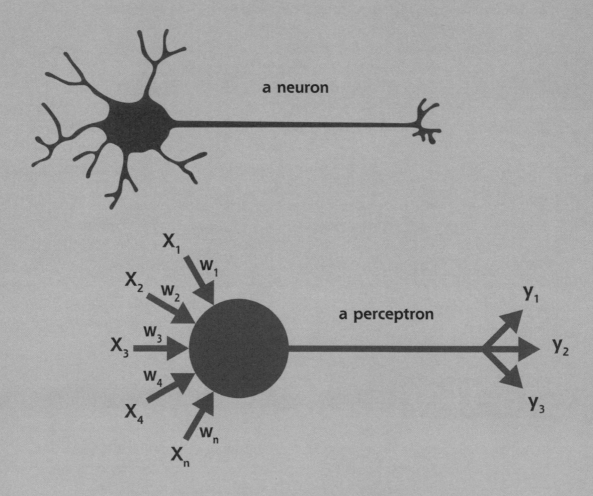

a neuron

a perceptron

The perceptron, as with all neural nets, adds another step. Each of the inputs is weighted, or given a value. Weights are usually between -1 and 1 and can be fractions. These weights tell the net's processor that one input might be more likely to be right than the others. For example, if the perceptron is learning to recognize cats, one input might be 90 percent likely to be a cat, while another might be 40 percent likely.

▶ Now you're going to do the math! Let's use these numbers to begin with.

$X_1 = 12$ $W_1 = 1$

$X_2 = 4$ $W_2 = \frac{1}{2}$

▶ Don't panic! Just plug in the numbers below. We'll ignore the activation step and the function for this exercise. And we'll use only two inputs.

1. Multiply the first input (X_1) by its weight (W_1).
   12 x 1 = 12

2. Multiply the second input (X_2) by its weight (W_2).
   4 x ½ = 2

3. Add the answers from steps 1 and 2 together.
   12 + 2 = 14

▶ Did you get 14?

Try This!

Vary the numbers of both the inputs and weights. Weights can be any fraction. How does the weight affect the output? You can also try adding more inputs if you're feeling daring!

MAKE A NEURAL NETWORK

A neural net is a series of connections in code. You can make a model of how a net handles information.

▶ **Stick three pushpins in a column** on the left side of a piece of cardboard. These are the inputs.

▶ **Stick four pushpins in a column in the middle** of the cardboard. These are the hidden layers. Leave enough room so that you can add more pins later.

▶ **Stick two pushpins in a column on the right side.** These are the outputs.

▶ **Tie one string from each input pin to each hidden layer pin.** Each input pin should have four strings coming from it.

▶ **Tie one string from each hidden layer pin to each output pin.** Each hidden layer pin should have two strings coming from it.

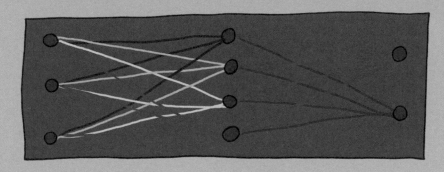

▶ **Now you have a model of a simple neural net!**

Next, try making the neural net deeper. You can add more rows of hidden layers and tie more string. How does this affect the flow of information?

DETECTING PATTERNS

When neural nets are trained to recognize something such as a cat or a number, they're really learning to look for patterns. Humans do this, too. We recognize a number 9, for instance, whether it's typed, handwritten, spray painted, or carved in stone. All of these look very different, but our brains look for a pattern. We see a loopy thing on the top and a straight line on the right and know it's a 9 without really thinking about it. Computers have a hard time with this, and that's why they need a lot of training data to learn how to recognize certain objects.

▶ **You're going to gather some training pictures and think about how to break them down into patterns.** Pick something relatively simple to begin with, such as a stop sign or a basketball.

▶ **With an adult's permission, gather a bunch of pictures of the object online or from magazines.** The pictures can be quite different. Some could be drawings, in a different language, and black-and-white, for instance.

▶ **Think about how you know what this object is when you see it.** What patterns do you look for? For example, stop signs are usually red, octagonal, and say, "Stop." Make a checklist of these patterns.

▶ **Look at each photo. Check off each pattern it meets.** Are there any photos that don't tick all the boxes, but you still know it's a stop sign? Why? How sure are you? For instance, the stop sign in the photo might be in Spanish, and you're 90 percent certain the word means *stop*.

Try This!

Now, find a more complicated object to train on. What patterns do you look for?

LEARN TO PLAY GO

After learning the rules, AlphaGo figured out how to play Go by watching championship players and playing millions of games against itself. You're going to try the same thing—and build your own Go board, called a goban. Most beginners start with a 9-by-9 grid, so that's what you'll be making!

❯ **On a piece of cardboard, draw a square that's 18 centimeters on each side.** Draw lines every 2 centimeters across and down to form a 9-by-9 grid. You should have nine squares across and down.

❯ **Mark the center of the grid with a small black circle.** Also mark the intersections of the second lines.

🔍 learn to play Go

❯ **Learn the rules of Go at this website. Watch a few games being played online.** Research some games on YouTube. You can even watch AlphaGo and AlphaGo Zero play each other. Here's the first game in that series.

🔍 AlphaGo Zero vs AlphaGo Master

❯ **Play a few games against yourself or an opponent.** Use coins or pebbles as your playing pieces. Take notes on strategies you learn as you play. What works? What doesn't? Note mistakes you made, too.

Consider This!

Reflect on what and how you learned. How might you avoid mistakes in the future? How do you think AlphaGo learns differently from you? Write a short paragraph or blog post about the experience.

DID YOU KNOW?

You can watch a Go game at this website. What can you learn from watching others play? Do AIs learn the same things as humans as they watch? Do you learn better by watching or doing?

🔍 Go board animated

Chapter 3

AI IN THE FUTURE

What will be the future of AI? Can you imagine having robot friends? Maybe scientists will develop robots that can rescue us from disaster and take care of us when we're old. Cars might take us where we want to go—without drivers. AIs might solve increasingly complex problems that affect the whole world, such as climate change. Or they might create works of art!

ESSENTIAL QUESTION

How might AI improve human lives in the future?

In some ways, the future is here. Researchers are already working on all these challenges—and more.

WORDS TO KNOW

roboticist: a scientist who researches, studies, and creates robots.

DARPA: The Defense Advanced Research Projects Agency (DARPA) is an agency of the U.S. Department of Defense responsible for the development of emerging technologies for use by the military.

social intelligence: the ability to get along well with others, and to get them to cooperate with you.

cue: a signal.

uncanny valley: when objects appear to be almost, but not quite, human, and spark feelings of discomfort.

ROBOTS

This century has seen a boom in robotics. We're still a long way from a fully thinking machine that can walk and talk. However, **roboticists** have made strides in the last decade in walking and other movement.

Early AI researchers didn't really view activities such as walking and grasping as intelligent activities. But roboticists discovered that movement is an essential feature of some robots and that walking—especially on two feet—is a very hard challenge to solve!

The First Robot Citizen

On October 25, 2017, Sophia became a citizen of Saudi Arabia. What's unusual about this? She is a social robot built by Hanson Robotics. Sophia is the first (and only) robot to be granted citizenship status in any country. Designed to look like actress Audrey Hepburn (1929–1993), Sophia is a life-like social robot capable of expressing and interpreting emotions.

credit: ITU Pictures from Geneva, Switzerland (CC BY 2.0)

 Watch Sophia being interviewed at the Future Investment Institute in Saudi Arabia. How does she differ from humans? Why do some humans want robots to display emotion? How does this make them useful?

🔎 CNBC interview Sophia

After the 2011 nuclear disaster in Fukushima, Japan, when a tsunami started a chain reaction that caused a nuclear accident, **DARPA** challenged roboticists to make humanoid robots that could rescue people and operate in disaster zones. DARPA is the Defense Advanced Research Projects Agency, the section of the U.S. Department of Defense responsible for the development of technologies for use by the military. You will learn more about the DARPA challenge in Chapter 4.

In addition to robots that can help in emergencies, roboticists are also developing robots with **social intelligence**. This includes the ability to interpret and express social **cues**, such as facial expressions, as well as knowing how to respond to humans. A social robot might be able to tell if a person is angry or sad. It might also be able to express emotions, at least to some extent.

This is a necessary skill when robots work closely with people. Humans feel more at ease working with more socially savvy robots.

Uncanny Valley

Designing the appearance of a social robot, or any robot, can be tricky. Humans need to feel comfortable interacting with it. If the robot is too cute, people tend to think of it as a toy and do not take it seriously. If the robot looks almost human, but not quite, then people tend to find the robot creepy. Humans feel better when a robot or an animated character looks exactly human—but that's extremely hard to do. Any look that falls short of that makes us uncomfortable. This uncomfortable zone is called the "**uncanny valley**." To avoid this, many robot designers tend to make humanoid robots more cartoonish, but with easy-to-recognize human features.

WORDS TO KNOW

dementia: a group of brain diseases that cause the gradual decline in a person's ability to think and remember.

autism spectrum: a group of developmental disorders that often includes difficulty communicating and interacting with others.

Several social robots are already on the market. Designed to identify emotions, a robot named Pepper has been used to greet customers in Japanese banks and other businesses. The robot can identify and adapt itself to emotions such as joy, sadness, and anger. For instance, if Pepper senses that you're sad, it will comfort you.

The same company that built Pepper also built NAO, a smaller social robot. As of 2017, more than 10,000 NAOs have been sold! NAOs have been used successfully in schools. Why do you think a socially adept robot might be useful in school?

Perhaps the brightest future for social robots is in caring for the elderly. In the United States, more than 10,000 people turn 65 every day. Yet there's a looming shortage of trained, human caregivers. Plus, in today's society, adult children often live far away from their aging parents. Do you live close to your grandparents?

Meet Paro!

Paro is not a stuffed animal. It is a therapy robot that looks like a white baby seal. Made by AIST, Paro has been dubbed the "world's most therapeutic robot" by the Guinness Book of World Records. Paro has been used in Europe and Japan since 2003. Research suggests that Paro is effective. It calms and engages older patients with **dementia**, for instance.

credit: Collision Conf (CC BY 2.0)

Three Wise Robots

In 2015, researchers at Rensselaer Polytechnic Institute gave three NAO robots a self-awareness test. It was based on a classic logic puzzle called the wise-men test. For the experiment, the roboticists disabled two of the three robots' ability to speak. They told the robots they were being given a pill that either made them unable to speak or a pill that did nothing. Then, the roboticists asked the robots which pill they got. All three robots considered the question for several seconds. Then one rose and said, "I don't know." Then the robot stopped itself and said "Sorry, I know now. . . ." The robot momentarily became self-aware!

You can watch the experiment at this website.

🔍 self-conscious NAO bots

Can you solve the original wise-men puzzle? It's a logic puzzle. Read the setup carefully.

The king called the three wisest men in all the land to his castle. He would pick one of them to become his new advisor—if that man passed this test. The king put a hat on each of the wise men's heads. They could see each other's hats but not their own. The king told them that (1) each hat was either blue or white, (2) at least one of them was wearing a blue hat, and (2) the test was fair to all of them. The wise men could not speak to each other. The king declared that the first one to stand up and correctly announce which color hat he was wearing would become the new advisor. Finally, one wise man rose and stated he was wearing a blue hat.

DID YOU KNOW?

Children on the **autism spectrum** respond well to robots! The NAO robot has been used successfully to help them learn to recognize emotions and communicate better.

Other countries have this problem, too. Japan's population is aging even faster than the U.S. population. By 2025, 30 percent of the Japanese population will be elderly, but the country will have only half the caregivers it needs. Therefore, many roboticists are developing robots to serve as companions and caregivers for the elderly. In fact, the Japanese government even set aside billions of yen in 2013 to fund research into caregiver robots!

DID YOU KNOW?

Robots played a role at the 2018 Winter Olympics in South Korea. Eighty robots were used to help visitors, clean venues, paint murals, and even ski!

These robots can provide a range of services, from companionship to light chores to full care. For example, ElliQ is a voice assistant similar to Alexa or Siri. However, she's designed specifically to interact with older people in their homes. ElliQ can remind its owner to take medication, eat, exercise, and so on. A robot assistant such as this can help older people stay independent and living in their own homes for a longer period.

Robots such as the Swedish GiraffPlus are tasked with many of the same jobs as ElliQ. GiraffPlus can vacuum, take **vital signs**, and provide video chat with doctors. Robear is a Japanese robot designed to lift patients out of beds and into wheelchairs. It can also help patients walk. Other researchers are working on robots that can dispense medicine, too.

A self-driving car at the DARPA Grand Challenge in 2005.
credit: Spaceape (CC BY 2.5)

An early self-driving car
credit: Travis Wise (CC BY 2.0)

SELF-DRIVING CARS

Science fiction is filled with cars that drive themselves. In that imaginary future, we summon a car and tell it our destination, and it whisks us away. We read a book or chat with a friend while the scenery rolls by. That future isn't very far off—but it's also not as close as people in past decades hoped it would be.

In the early 2000s, DARPA challenged engineers to build a practical, self-driving vehicle. Teams across the world built cars that were meant to drive themselves on a closed course. The first competition, held in 2004, was not a success. None of the cars finished the course.

Later challenges were more successful—even though the courses were much more difficult. In 2005, cars had to drive over a narrow, winding road. In 2007, the cars had to navigate urban streets on a closed military base. Following these challenges, an engineer from one of the winning teams joined Google Research, which later developed the first practical, self-driving car.

WORDS TO KNOW

autonomous: acting independently.

semi-autonomous: acting independently to some degree.

radar: a device that detects objects by bouncing radio waves off them and measuring how long it takes for the waves to return.

lidar: a device that measures distance by shining light at an object and measuring the time it takes for the light to reflect back.

infrastructure: the basic physical and organizational structures and facilities, such as buildings, roads, and power supplies, needed for the operation of a society or enterprise.

Today, self-driving—or **autonomous**—cars are already on the road in a few places. For example, in Phoenix, Arizona, the company Waymo (formerly known as the Google self-driving project) has launched a trial program for commuters to try out its self-driving vehicles.

In Pittsburgh, Pennsylvania, and Tempe, Arizona, Uber users can take advantage of an autonomous ride. Uber—the ride-sharing company—has worked with Volvo to produce a small fleet of self-driving cars. A human driver, however, is behind the wheel just in case. The driver can take over in the event of a problem.

Most automakers are developing their own self-driving models as well as continuing to introduce **semi-autonomous** safety features in new cars. Tesla, for instance, is equipping its new cars with self-driving hardware—but not necessarily the software.

Waymo's Carcraft

One way to teach a self-driving AI is on the road. Another way is through simulation. Waymo has developed a simulation called Carcraft, named after the online game Warcraft. Originally, Waymo designed Carcraft to play back scenes when the AI encountered something new—such as a rotary—in the real world. Programmers soon realized they could train the AI virtually using accurate 3-D maps of cities and test tracks. Plus, they could train many virtual self-driving cars at once. At any one time, 25,000 virtual cars are running simulations in Carcraft and can rack up millions of miles of virtual driving every day.

The future is almost here for AI-driven cars. Almost.

As of 2018, experts say that fully autonomous cars are about 85 to 90 percent here, technologically speaking. But getting to 100 percent or even 96 percent might take years—decades even. Why? Some of the toughest issues still need to be solved. The technology challenges include better sensors, more accurate mapping, and the AI software itself.

Today's self-driving cars have bulky sensors mounted on top of the car and elsewhere. This gives the car a 360-degree view of its surroundings. Autonomous cars use **radar** and **lidar** to scan the road for objects. Radar uses high-frequency radio waves and lidar uses lasers to detect objects. These sensors, as well as onboard cameras, can sense the road, lanes, other vehicles, pedestrians, and cyclists.

Today's self-driving cars can sense their immediate surroundings. Tomorrow's self-driving cars, though, will also need to communicate with other cars and the **infrastructure** itself.

DID YOU KNOW?

The automaker Tesla has had problems with its self-driving program, called Autopilot. In 2016, a passenger was killed when a self-driven car failed to brake after a truck turned in front of it.

WORDS TO KNOW

GPS: also called Global Positioning System, a radio navigation system that allows land, sea, and airborne users to determine their exact location, velocity, and time 24 hours a day, in all weather conditions, anywhere in the world.

virtual: a computer version of something real.

This communication will ensure that cars flow smoothly, avoiding traffic jams, accidents, and even icy bridges or flooded roads. Some carmakers today are including radio systems for this. For instance, one car model can connect to a smart stoplight. Most of our infrastructure, however, isn't "smart." Yet.

Mapping is another area that needs to improve. Today's cars have **GPS** and mapping systems. But GPS is only accurate to within 6½ feet. This works well for finding a new friend's house. But a self-driving car needs a much more accurate view of the world to drive down a busy street or along a narrow, winding mountain road! Engineers are working on developing highly accurate maps that can be navigated using lidar and radar.

The biggest gap in technology is the AI itself. The AIs today just don't have enough driving experience. They're like teenagers learning to drive! They're trustworthy in certain areas or under direct supervision, but they might not know how to handle some emergency situations. Some of these situations are ones you might see every day or only once in a lifetime, such as a tree crashing into the road or a car drifting into the wrong lane or failing to stop at a red light. The AI software under the hood can sense vehicles, roads, and pedestrians, but the software doesn't understand driver behavior.

A basic GPS mapping system will help you find your way to a new place, but it's not always super accurate.

Self-Driving Semis

Self-driving cars get all the press. Quietly, companies such as Daimler, Tesla, Google, and Uber have also been designing self-driving semi-trucks. For example, in 2015, Daimler unveiled the first self-driving commercial truck licensed in a U.S. state (Nevada). Called the Freightliner Inspiration, it is not entirely autonomous. A human driver has to be in the driver's seat. They control the truck on streets and roads. On the highway, though, the driver can turn on the Highway Pilot feature. The Inspiration is equipped with radar and camera systems as well as adaptive cruise control. In self-drive mode, the semi will stay in its lane and keep a safe distance from other traffic.

Designers are working on programming the AI to use machine learning to handle these situations. For example, Waymo is training its AI to understand and predict other driver behavior by exposing it to millions of miles of driving experience. This, of course, takes time.

Waymo and other autonomous car designers are using different techniques to give AIs more experience at a faster rate. Ford's test fleet of self-driving Fusions share information with each other. Tesla uses data from its human drivers to improve its software. Waymo uses a computer simulation called Carcraft to give its AI **virtual** driving experience.

Technological gaps are not the only hurdles autonomous cars have to face. According to recent surveys, Americans have serious concerns and even fears about AI-controlled cars. Three out of four drivers surveyed by the American Automobile Association (AAA) said they'd be afraid to ride in a self-driving car. Most trust their own driving skills over an AI's.

DID YOU KNOW? Lidar isn't just for cars! It was first used in the 1960s to map clouds. In 1971, the crew of *Apollo 15* used lidar to map the moon's surface! Today, a network of observatories on Earth uses lidar to accurately measure the distance to the moon. Lidar is also used for weather, mapping, archaeology, and many other fields.

Some people were even reluctant to try semi-autonomous features offered on many new cars. These include collision avoidance, self-parking, and automatic emergency braking. Most people surveyed didn't want to give up control of their cars. At the very least, they wanted the ability to take over at any time.

How would you feel riding in a self-driving car? Would you be comfortable giving up control to a machine?

Drivers who already had used semi-autonomous safety features on their cars, though, were more likely to trust the technology and want to have it on their next cars. These people might be more open to fully autonomous cars. The semi-autonomous safety features could serve as stepping stones toward truly autonomous cars in the future. But so far, the public and lawmakers have been reluctant to embrace self-driving cars, at least until more research has been done.

Levels of Car Autonomy

1	Driver assistance	Human is in full control, car can take over one or more functions
2	Partial autonomy	Human driver is still responsible but car can take over steering, braking, accelerating
3	Conditional autonomy	Car can drive on its own, but human must pay attention and can take over
4	High autonomy	Human hands over control in certain situations, such as highway driving
5	Full autonomy	Car controls itself under all conditions

Self-Driving Accidents

Unfortunately, autonomous cars have been in a few accidents. In March 2018, a self-driving Uber hit and killed a pedestrian in Arizona. The accident happened even with a driver behind the wheel. This was the first fatality involving a self-driving car, but not the first accident. Google's autonomous vehicle (AV) fleet has been in numerous fender-benders over the years. However, only in one instance was the car itself at fault. In 2016, a Google AV hit the side of a bus at very low speed. Do you think self-driving cars have a place in society? Why or why not?

CREATIVE AI

The ultimate act of intelligence might just be creativity. Can an AI compose a song or write a story? Maybe. Some researchers have used AI algorithms to create movie trailers, paintings, songs, and other creative works—with varying degrees of success.

IBM's Watson, for example, made a trailer for a film called *Morgan*, an AI horror movie. Watson analyzed hundreds of trailers for similar movies. Then, it drew scenes from these trailers.

In the end, a human editor put the trailer together, but Watson greatly reduced the time needed to make it.

Watch Watson's Trailer

Watch the *Morgan* trailer and learn how Watson helped make it.

PS How do you think it's different from what a human would have done?

🔍 Morgan trailer

Launched in 2016, Google's Magenta Project is also exploring the possibilities of AI creation. Magenta is learning to compose music and paint pictures using machine learning.

Magenta listens to or looks at examples of art and then tries to create its own.

Right now, Watson and Magenta may not be truly creating art, but they may help humans to be more creative. Do you think having an AI assistant would help you be creative? Do you think it would limit your creativity? How?

These are just a few of the areas AI might go in the next few years. Beyond that, the future is hard to predict! Often, breakthroughs come in unexpected ways.

Play a Duet with an AI

Built using Google's Magenta Project code, this experiment lets you play a virtual duet with an AI. You don't even need to know how to play the piano! Just click some keys and the AI responds.

Learn more about the project at this site.

🔍 learn about AI duet

PS **You can play with it yourself at this site.**

🔍 learn about AI duet

And, as you'll find out in the next chapter, not everyone agrees whether the future of AI holds great promise or great danger.

Rufus the Nomad office dog appears in one photograph that is unaltered and one that has been reworked by an AI program. Which do you think is cuter?

ESSENTIAL QUESTION

How might AI improve human lives in the future?

EXPLORING THE UNCANNY VALLEY

Humans can be uncomfortable working with robots that look almost, but not quite, like humans. For some reason this becomes strange and frightening. You're going to design an experiment to see how people react to different types of robots.

❯ **Think about the questions you want to answer with this experiment.** What hypothesis do you want to test? For example, you might hypothesize that people prefer to work with human-looking robots. You'll need three friends or classmates to serve as testers.

❯ **Collect and print out five images of robots.** You can find these on the internet, with an adult's permission, or in magazines. The images should range from very human-like to very cartoonish. Be sure to include at least one creepy one that falls into the uncanny valley category. The robots can be real or from movies, television, or video games.

❯ **In your engineering notebook, write a few questions you'd like the testers to answer.** For instance, which robot do they prefer to work or play with and why? How does the robot's appearance make them feel? There's no right or wrong question or answer.

❯ **Ask your testers your questions while showing them the pictures.** If they give permission, you can record their reactions.

❯ **Analyze your data!** Which photo did most people pick? Why? What do you think your results say about how humans see robots?

Try This!

Write a short paragraph summarizing your results. You can also make a graph to better see your data. What conclusions can you come to?

CRAFTING THE UNCANNY VALLEY

You're going to create a three-dimensional (3-D) robot face that's like yours—almost. You'll tweak it a bit here and there to get it to fall within the uncanny valley. Just how creepy can you make it? How are people going to react?

❯ **Take a photo of your full face.** Print it out on plain white paper. Make the printout as large or a bit larger than your actual face! Cut out holes for your eyes.

❯ **Build your robot face mask.** Using the photo as a guide, lay clay or playdough down on the paper. Try to use materials that match your skin and lip color. You might need to look at the photo on your computer or in a mirror as you build your robot mask. Try to get it as realistic as possible. Sculpt the nose, lips, eyebrows, and cheekbones out of the appropriate colors. (You don't need to do your hair.)

❯ **Hold the robot face over yours and look in the mirror.** How does the face make you feel? If it's very like your own, it might creep you out! If so, you've entered the uncanny valley!

❯ **Tweak the features of your face.** What happens if the lips are too big or the nose is pointier?

❯ **Now, try making a mask with more cartoonish features.** For instance, you could make the skin lime green or the features very simple. Is this version less creepy? Would you want to work or play with a robot with this face? Why?

Try This!

Take photos of each of the masks you make. Have a friend or family member look at the pictures and pick the creepiest. Caption each with the changes you made and rate where it falls in the uncanny valley:
1 for super creepy to 5 for super cute.

WORDS TO KNOW

three-dimensional (3-D): an image that has length, width, and height, and is raised off the flat page.

MEME THE FUTURE!

What do you think the future of artificial intelligence will be? What would you like it to be? You're going to be the expert—and share your predictions.

❯ **Do some research. What have experts said about the future of AI?** Very often, magazines such as *Wired* or *Forbes* or *MIT Technology Review* feature experts predicting the future of the field. With an adult's permission, find a few of those articles online or at the library. What do the experts think? Do you agree? Why or why not?

❯ **Do a bit more research. What are some exciting areas in AI right now?** What do you think they'll be like in a few years? You might want to narrow your search a bit. For instance, what's the future of social robots? Or self-driving cars? Or AI in health care or cybercrime?

❯ **Make your own predictions.** Write them down in your engineering notebook. Why do you think each one will come about?

❯ **Now make a meme about one or more of your predictions.** A meme is a popular and entertaining item, such as a captioned picture. Find a photo or picture that best captures your prediction and caption it with a quote from you about the future of AI.

Try This!

Share this meme with friends and family. Do they agree with your prediction? Why or why not? Explain the evidence that backs up your prediction.

WORDS TO KNOW

meme: an amusing or interesting item such as a captioned picture or video that is spread widely online, especially through social media.

MAKE A ROBOT

You can make a pretty simple robot in your classroom or at home! Let's try making a robot that draws pictures. For this project, you'll need an electric toothbrush and a section of pool noodle. Have an adult help you cut through the foam.

❯ **Put batteries in the toothbrush and remove the brush end of the toothbrush.** You just need the motor inside the toothbrush to power your robot.

❯ **Cut a section of the pool noodle that's a little longer than the toothbrush.** Discard the rest of the noodle or save it to use to make more robots!

❯ **Tape one marker to the side of the noodle, with the marker point down.** About one-third of the marker should be below the bottom of the noodle.

❯ **Repeat this step for two more markers.** Each should be placed about one-third of the way around the noodle, forming a tripod.

❯ **Lower the toothbrush (brush side down) into the hole in the noodle.** Leave the on/off button exposed. Tape the toothbrush in place.

❯ **Remove the marker caps** and place your robot on a sheet of paper.

DID YOU KNOW?

What happens when an AI tries to give a pep talk? Read some inspiring quotes generated by an AI.

"It's never too late to be yourself."

"Birds will control wealth."

"Without a leaf, there can be no lobster."

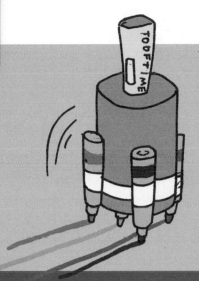

▶ **Turn it on and let your robot create!** It should move around, leaving patterns on the paper. If it doesn't, try adjusting the placement of the markers. Experiment with different marker colors, too.

Consider This!

Do you think this robot is making art? Why or why not? What do you think of your robot-drawn creations. Are they visually pleasing? Do you like them?

Van Google? Leonardo da Virtual? Machine-Angelo?

If robots are able to be creative and produce works of art that people hang in their homes to enjoy and be inspired by, what does that mean for human creativity? There's always a worry that AI will replace humans, whether it's the people whose jobs are replaced by the self-checkout machines at the grocery store or writers who fear AI will get really good at generating plots and characters for books. Is there any way that human artists will be completely replaced by AI artists? Art has long been considered to be an outlet for the pain, joy, confusion, and wonderment that are shared emotions among all humans, but as Watson and Magenta get better at producing art and music, we could find that what we thought of as uniquely human can actually be experienced by machines. What effect might this have on human art?

MAKE A BUGBOT

Robot designers often look to nature for inspiration. They've even designed robots that move, fly, and communicate like insects. For example, researchers at Harvard University designed RoboBee, a tiny bot that flies like a bee. You, too, can make your own bug-inspired bot! You'll need a few special supplies, including a 1.5- to 3-volt mini motor, often called a hobby motor, as well as a AA single battery holder with leads, AA battery, and foam board.

PS Check out RoboBee at this website!

🔍 RoboBee

❯ **Attach the bottom of the battery holder to the flat side of the motor.** Tip: Leave the contacts exposed so you can attach the wires! If you don't have a battery holder, cut out a small piece of foam board, no wider or longer than the motor. Glue the foam board to the top of the motor. Then glue the battery to the motor.

❯ **Unbalance the motor.** Cut out and glue a small piece of foam board to the tip of the motor shaft. You can also use an eraser or anything else that unbalances the motor. Unbalancing the motor creates a wobble, which makes the bugbot move.

❯ **Attach the wires from the battery holder to the leads of the motor.** You can twist the ends of the wires onto the leads.

❯ **Add legs!** Cut out a small piece of foam board and glue it to the bottom of the motor. This will make it easier to attach legs. You can bend the ends of large paperclips and stick them into the foam board. Glue or tape them to make the legs more secure. Experiment with other materials, too.

➤ **Decorate!** You can add eyes or other items to your bugbot.

➤ **Insert the battery—and let it go.** The bugbot should vibrate and move. If not, try adjusting the legs or unbalancing the motor more.

➤ **Take a picture or video of your bugbot** and share it!

Try This!

Make another bugbot, but this time vary the design. What happens if you use something else for the legs?

Robotic Insects

"How many RoboBees have we crashed? All of them." Robert Wood, a *National Geographic* 2014 Emerging Explorer and award-winning engineer, is working to develop robotic insects! Why do we need more bugs in the world? They can work to get information to emergency responders at disaster sites. They might also be useful for agriculture as climate change alters weather patterns and growing seasons.

 You can watch a short video about robotic insects at this site.

🔎 Nat Geo Robotic Bees

SELF-DRIVING CARS TODAY

Many of today's cars have features that use AI or demonstrate a low level of self-driving. Your family might already have a car with collision warnings or self-parking, for example. How close are we to having self-driving cars today? You're going to do some research to find out! A good starting place is a *Consumer Reports* feature on self-driving cars. You can find it at this website.

🔍 Consumer Reports self-driving cars

❯ **Research the companies that make fully autonomous cars today.** For example, as of 2018, Tesla and Waymo have produced self-driving cars. Who else has? Are major car companies working on self-driving cars? What's stopping people from adopting fully autonomous cars? For example, are they legal in every state?

❯ **What features do new cars have that include some amount of AI?** One example is the ability for a car to parallel park itself. Make a list of these features. Which cars have them?

❯ **Make an infographic or chart to show your findings.** For instance, list carmakers on the left side and the features across the top. Include fully autonomous as one of the features. Add a check mark if a carmaker has that AI feature.

Try This!

Pick one or more of the features you researched, such as self-parking. Do a little more research. Do your parents and any other adults you know have a car with one of these features? Do they use and like the feature? Why or why not?

Chapter 4

DO WE NEED AI?

> THERE'S SOME AI THAT I WOULD HAVE A HARD TIME LIVING WITHOUT!

> YEAH — LIKE CHESSTR!

> AND IF WE COULDN'T PREDICT DISASTERS, IT COULD BE – –

> DISASTROUS!!

> I WALKED RIGHT INTO THAT.

As humans, we've dreamed for centuries about building thinking machines. And we've built some amazing computers and robots. But do we really need them?

ESSENTIAL QUESTION

What might today's world be like without the influence of AI?

Of course, humans have survived just fine for centuries without AI, but it has many benefits, some of which you've probably already picked up on. Here are just a few more.

WORDS TO KNOW

meltdown: an uncontrolled reaction in a nuclear power plant.

evacuate: to leave a dangerous place to go to a safe place.

radiation: a form of electromagnetic energy that can cause harm to humans and other living creatures, as well as a form of treatment for diseases such as cancer.

gravity: the force that pulls objects toward each other and holds you on Earth.

asteroid: a small rocky body that circles around the sun.

dwarf planet: an astronomical object that is smaller than a planet and orbits the sun.

interstellar: existing or occurring between stars.

NASA: the National Aeronautics and Space Administration, the United States organization in charge of space exploration.

habitat: a plant or animal's home, which supplies it with food, water, and shelter.

SAFETY

On March 11, 2011, a 9.1 magnitude earthquake off the coast of Japan triggered a tsunami—and a nuclear **meltdown** at the Fukushima Daiichi power plant. Thousands of people died because of flooding, and the area around Fukushima had to be **evacuated**.

Shortly after this disaster, roboticists begin to ask themselves: What if we'd had robots to help rescue people?

Humanoid and other kinds of robots could easily go into places that aren't safe for humans. DARPA issued a challenge to build search-and-rescue robots who could think for themselves, at least to some degree.

Many teams of engineers took up the challenge, building 25 robots for the finals. They had to compete against each other on a series of obstacle courses. In the final challenge in 2015, robots had to drive a car, climb stairs, use power tools, walk through rubble, and so forth. The winning teams received millions of dollars to further develop their robots.

Robots and, to some extent, AI, can go boldly where humans can't or don't want to go. Think about space exploration. Most space missions have been robotic. Why?

DID YOU KNOW?

Drones can be used to fly over disaster sites and find survivors. One problem, though, is something called disaster tourism, which is when amateur drone users fly their own machines and get in the way of those from rescue units.

Space is a hazardous place, full of extreme temperatures and **radiation**, and with little **gravity** and oxygen. Plus, it takes a very long time to get anywhere in space since everything is so far away from everything else!

It makes sense to send robotic spacecraft to other planets, **asteroids**, **dwarf planets,** moons, the sun, and even **interstellar** space. We also use robots to work outside the International Space Station. Most of these robotic craft have limited or no AI. **NASA**, however, is developing a humanoid robot named Valkyrie to send to Mars.

Its mission will be to build a **habitat** for human astronauts before they arrive. The robot would then work alongside the astronaut crew as it explores the Red Planet.

DARPA Robotics Challenge Finals

May the best robot win! The finals of the DARPA challenge to build search-and-rescue robots were held in June 2015 in Pomona, California.

You can watch the whole competition on DARPA's YouTube channel and check the outcomes on its website.

🔍 DARPA 2015

PS **Watch the 2015 finals on DARPAtv.**

🔍 DARPA 2015 video

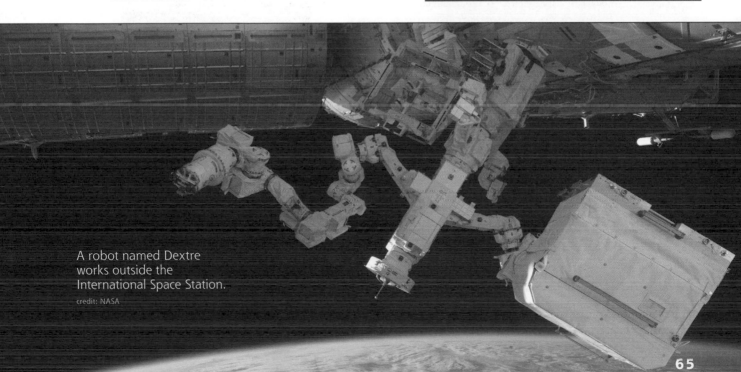

A robot named Dextre works outside the International Space Station.
credit: NASA

WORDS TO KNOW

skeptical: questioning and not easily convinced.

carbon emissions: the release of carbon dioxide and other carbon gases into the atmosphere.

Another safety example is the self-driving car that we discussed in the last chapter. Driving doesn't seem quite as dangerous as space exploration or search-and-rescue missions, but about 3,000 people a day worldwide die in automobile accidents! More than 33,000 of those deaths happen in the United States every year. According to the National Highway Traffic Safety Administration (NHTSA), human error is the critical reason for 94 percent of car crashes. What's the solution? Take the human out of the driver's seat. These are the statistics most car makers point out when talking about self-driving cars.

Meet Valkyrie

In 2016, NASA challenged research teams to develop software for Valkyrie, also known as R5. The goal of the Space Robotics Challenge was to increase Valkyrie's ability to operate on her own. That way, she could complete tasks during space travel and after landing on Mars—without much human supervision. The challenge involved programming a virtual R5 to complete a series of complex tasks on Mars. For instance, Valkyrie had to deal with the aftermath of a dust storm and repair its damage. More than 400 teams entered! The final competition in 2017 was won by a one-man team.

credit: NASA

PS NASA's R5 robot, nicknamed Valkyrie, is NASA's newest humanoid robot. It was built to compete in the DARPA Robotics Challenge and advance the state of robotics within the agency. **Check R5 out at this website.**

🔎 NASA Valkyrie video

Google self-driving car
credit: Steve Jurvetson (CC BY 2.0)

Once fully autonomous driving is achieved, most experts believe transportation will be safer. AIs can't be distracted by their phones! Also, they'll never drink and drive. However, at this point in autonomous car development, human drivers, consumer groups, and NHTSA are **skeptical** about the ability of current self-driving cars to be safer.

DID YOU KNOW?

Ford plans to sell fully autonomous ride-sharing cars by 2021. The cars won't have steering wheels or pedals.

Self-driving cars might also contribute to a cleaner environment and reduced **carbon emissions**. According the Union of Concerned Scientists, transportation is responsible for more than half of air pollution. Self-driving cars will help eliminate traffic congestion, cutting down carbon and pollution emissions. Plus, some companies, such as Tesla, are developing electric self-driving cars, which will be better for the environment since they won't burn fossil fuels.

DID YOU KNOW?

Approved in 2000 for use in the United States, da Vinci robots do approximately 400,000 surgeries a year.

ROBOTIC SURGERY

Robots are also lifesavers in medicine, even though they can't operate by themselves yet! Surgical and medical robots give the human doctor better control. The most widely used robot is the da Vinci Surgical System.

The da Vinci has four robotic arms, each with tiny surgical tools or cameras. Its 3-D cameras give the doctor a high-definition, 3-D view of the surgical site. The surgeon controls the robot from a console, using hand controllers to move the scalpel or laser. The robot's software smooths out the surgeon's hand movements.

The da Vinci enables doctors to perform delicate, complicated surgeries that might not be possible otherwise.

Some medical robots are even more automated. CyberKnife, for instance, is a fully robotic system for treating cancer with radiation. Using real-time imaging, the robot can pinpoint cancer cells with high doses of radiation and even adjust itself if the patient moves. Other surgical robots perform different medical procedures. Medicine is an area that can continue to improve with the help of AI!

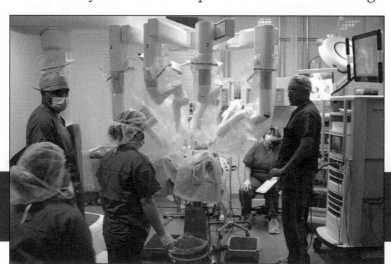

The da Vinci Xi at the Keesler Medical Center
credit: U.S. Air Force

BIONICS

Scientists are now building **bionic** limbs with machine intelligence. With most artificial limbs, such as legs, the wearer must think carefully about how to move their leg and set the foot down on the ground. Walking can be a whole new experience.

The first bionic limb available on the market, Össur's Symbionic Leg, "thinks" for its wearer. Sensors in the artificial leg read tiny changes in body position and scan the terrain below. Computer chips pick the best angle to swing the foot forward and put it on the ground. The leg can even help wearers stay upright when they stumble!

Army Staff Sgt. Billy Costello stretches and flexes his bionic ankle, which he received after losing his leg by stepping on an explosive device.

credit: DOD photo by Terri Moon Cronk

No More Vacuuming or Lawn Mowing!

If you don't enjoy household chores, robotic help is on the way! Many companies now make robotic vacuum cleaners. These run by themselves and can avoid obstacles such as furniture—although stairs are still a challenge. Some can even be controlled remotely with a smartphone while you are away from home! While they don't work quite as well—yet—as normal vacuum cleaners, and are very expensive, they are constantly improving. Robotic lawn mowers are also becoming available to help with another task that many people hate. Although many of these lawn mowers can handle only small yards, some can handle up to one acre at a time! And just like vacuum cleaners, they can be controlled from a smartphone. Which of your chores would you like to see roboticized?

EXOSKELETONS

Exoskeletons are another way robotics are helping people walk. An exoskeleton is a wearable robot that fits over a person's legs and **torso**. The exoskeleton senses small shifts in the person's weight. Then, motors flex the exoskeleton's hips and knees to make the person move. ReWalk was one of the first exoskeletons approved for home use. Other exoskeletons, such as Ekso, are mostly used for physical therapy. They help people with spinal cord or brain injuries learn how to walk again.

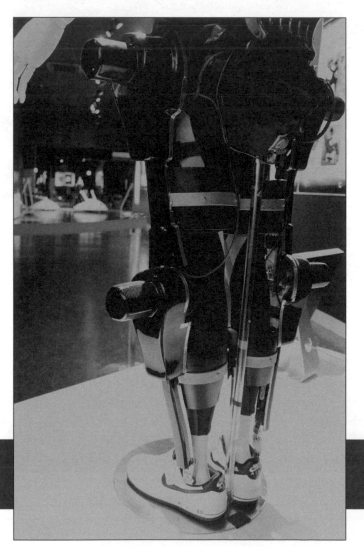

DID YOU KNOW?

In 2012, a paralyzed woman named Claire Lomas finished the London Marathon wearing a ReWalk exoskeleton. It took her 17 days to cross the finish line!

A robotics device designed to help people walk, from the company Cyberdyne
credit: Yuichiro C. Katsumoto (CC BY 2.0)

WORKING SMARTER

Have you sent a snapchat, taken a photo, uploaded your English essay, or watched a video online today? In today's world, we are drowning in data. An immense amount of information is being stored and exchanged, too much information for us to control.

AI can help us handle all that data so we can work smarter. An AI is very good at sifting through enormous amounts of information and finding the connections. Medicine is one area that's especially in need of help from AI. For example, IBM's Watson helps doctors make diagnoses. Most doctors don't have the time to keep up with all the new research published in medical journals every year. But Watson can! The AI can search all the journals and databases and then make suggestions for treatment.

AIs such as Watson also work with tax preparers to help them keep changes in tax laws straight. AIs help insurance companies analyze claims. And they find and predict hacking attempts and other **cyberthreats**, to name just a few areas.

WORDS TO KNOW

veteran: someone who has served in the military.

psychological: pertaining to or relating to the mind.

HUMAN CONNECTION

Amazingly, AI research helps us understand ourselves. Building a thinking machine makes us consider what it means to be intelligent. Building a social machine also forces us to look at emotions and social cues.

To improve how machines and robots interact with humans and vice versa, AIs need to learn to sense and react appropriately to emotions. To figure this out, AI researchers must learn a lot about how humans sense and react, too. We pick up emotions and other cues from faces and body language. By focusing on these aspects of being human, we gain more understanding of ourselves and others, even as we work closely with nonhumans.

DID YOU KNOW?

IBM's Watson has also helped Guiding Eyes for the Blind pair dogs with trainers. The organization put hundreds of thousands of dogs' health and training records online. Watson dug through the data to find patterns to help more dogs graduate and become guide dogs for the blind!

And sometimes people would rather work with a robot!

Take Ellie, for instance. Ellie is a virtual therapist. She interviews **veterans** and identifies **psychological** problems. Many vets are often reluctant to admit problems to other humans, and they've found it easier to talk to Ellie.

DeepMind

In 2017, Google's DeepMind developed an AI that taught itself to walk, run, and jump—virtually, that is! The AI had never seen what walking looks like. Its first attempts at movement are goofy but still very effective!

PS **Watch it at this website.**

🔍 DeepMind walking

A seeing eye dog that is now used to train other dogs in the Guiding Eyes for the Blind program, which Watson helps to organize

credit: U.S. Air Force photo/Jason Minto

Likewise, elderly patients in Japan have found robotic caretakers less stressful than human ones. Japan's population is growing older, yet its nursing workforce is shrinking. Researchers hope that robots can fill that void in years to come.

AIs are very useful in many different areas of our lives. So, why aren't there more of them? Why don't companies spend more time and money creating new robots and improving older ones? Part of this answer has to do with the reluctance some people have to dive into the AI world. We'll learn more about some of the anxiety people have about AI in the next chapter.

ESSENTIAL QUESTION

What might today's world be like without the influence of AI?

DESIGN A RESCUE ROBOT

The DARPA challenge was all about designing robots that can respond to disasters. You're going to design your own!

❯ **First, think about what the robot needs to do! Do some research.** Watch the videos of the DARPA challenge and find out more about other robots designed for hazardous conditions, such as space. What kind of conditions do these robots need to operate in? What tasks do the robots perform?

❯ **Come up with a list of skills and other requirements for your robot.** For instance, does it need to climb steps? Use tools? Be waterproof? Think for itself? You'll use this as a checklist for your design!

❯ **Next, sketch your robot in your engineering notebook.** Label and describe its features. How does each feature enable your robot to do something on your checklist? Which feature do you think would be the trickiest to build and why?

Curiosity

Valkyrie is not quite ready for Mars, but the *Curiosity* rover is already there and hard at work. It landed on the Red Planet in August 2012.

 You can take the virtual *Curiosity* rover for a spin at this site!

🔍 experience curiosity

Try This!

Build a model of your robot! You can use any materials for this. How would you improve your design?

DESIGN A SPACE ROBOT

NASA's Valkyrie started out as a contestant in the DARPA Robotics Challenge. Now, NASA wants to send Valkyrie to Mars to prepare the way for human astronauts. However, R5 won't be the first robot in space. Far from it. Several other robotic craft have already explored Mars, and a few robots are working on the International Space Station right now. You're going to design your own space robot.

❱ **First, think about what the robot needs to do!** Do you want a robot that explores Mars? How about one that works on a space station or the moon?

❱ **Do some research on current space robots.** NASA Robotics is a good starting place.

❱ **Investigate the conditions in which the robots might have to operate and the tasks they might need to perform.** For missions to other planets, moons, or asteroids, start with the NASA Solar System site. If you're interested in space stations, check out the International Space Station.

❱ **Come up with a list of skills and other requirements for your robot.** For instance, does it need to work in zero gravity? Mine asteroids? Think for itself? You'll use this as a checklist for your design!

❱ **Next, sketch your robot.** Label and describe its features. How does each enable your robot to do something on your checklist? Which feature do you think would be the trickiest to build and why?

Try This!

Build a model of your robot! You can use any materials for this. What kinds of problems do you need to solve to make it useful in space?

SPOT AN ALGORITHM IN THE WILD

AI algorithms are all around us, usually performing very specific tasks. For instance, they're reminding us it's time to leave for soccer practice, recommending movies to us on a video streaming site, searching for information on the internet, picking out a new song to play for us, or predicting what we want to buy next.

With an adult's permission, see how many algorithms you can spot on the internet!

❱ **Pick a music or video streaming site,** such as Pandora, YouTube, or Netflix.

❱ **Do a little research on how the site works.** For instance, you can search for articles on how Netflix's algorithms work. How do they predict what you'll want to watch? How do they keep track of what you've already watched?

❱ **Next, go to the site and poke around a bit.** How many algorithms can you spot? For instance, does the site tell you what's popular or trending? Does it give you suggestions? Are they based on things you've watched or listened to in the past? Make a list of the possible algorithms being used.

❱ **What else do you observe?** Do the algorithms work the way you'd like them to? Why or why not? For instance, do they really recommend movies or music you like? Write a short paragraph detailing what you found out from your research and exploration of algorithms.

Try This!

Try another site and compare how its algorithms work.

DESIGN A CAREGIVER OR COMPANION ROBOT

Our population is aging, yet we might have a shortage of human healthcare workers to care for the elderly. Some roboticists are designing social and caregiver robots especially for older people. Design a robot as either a companion or a caregiver for an elderly person.

❯ **First, think about what the robot needs to do!** Do you want a robot that keeps an older person company? Does the robot need to care for a person with a disability? Would it work in a person's home, a hospital, or somewhere else?

❯ **With an adult's permission, do some research on current social robots,** particularly those designed with older people in mind. This article in *Robotics Tomorrow* is a good place to start.

🔍 Robotics Tomorrow caregiver

❯ **Investigate the conditions the robot might have to operate** in and the tasks it might have to do. Would your robot be doing chores in a home? Would your robot be acting as an orderly in a nursing home?

❯ **Come up with a list of skills and other requirements for your robot.** For instance, does it need to lift 300 pounds? Tell jokes? Remind someone to take their medications? Think for itself? You'll use this as a checklist for your design!

❯ **Next, sketch your robot.** Label and describe its features. How does each enable your robot to do something on your checklist? Which feature do you think would be the trickiest to build and why? How would a caregiver robot for a child differ from one for your great-grandmother?

Try This!

Come up with other service robots that would be useful to humans. What problems might be solved with an AI?

Chapter 5

AI IN
SCIENCE FICTION

AI IS ALL OVER THE MEDIA, TOO – WE SEE IT EVERY DAY!

ROBO-WORLD

AI CAN BE REALLY SCARY IN MOVIES AND THINGS. THEY CAN EVEN BE THE BAD GUYS!

WELL, WE USE THINGS LIKE AI IN MEDIA TO EXPLORE OUR FEARS. THEY'RE EASY TO BE AFRAID OF!

OH – LIKE A METAPHOR!

Thinking machines have lived in people's imaginations for thousands of years. We've told stories about bringing **inanimate** figures to life. We've written books, plays, movies, comic books, and television shows with AI and robots as characters.

Technology in science fiction is usually many years, even decades, ahead of reality. But our stories often reflect the concerns and fears of the time in which the stories were told.

ESSENTIAL QUESTION

How do science fiction movies and books reflect our attitudes toward robots and AI in the real world?

FROM ANCIENT TIMES TO THE NINETEENTH CENTURY

Most **mythologies** include stories of mechanical "men." In Greek myth, Hephaestus—the god of fire, metalworking, and stone masonry—made talking handmaidens out of gold. In *The Iliad*, the epic poem about the **Trojan War**, Hephaestus made mechanical creatures to serve the gods. *The Iliad* was written more than 3,000 years ago!

Another example of robot mythology is the golem. In Jewish folklore, a golem is a clay man. It's brought to life when sacred words written on a slip of paper are placed in the golem's mouth. Removing the words causes the golem to slump back to sleep. In early stories, the golem is usually a servant who is too mechanical in fulfilling his master's wishes. By the sixteenth century, golems in stories became the protectors of Jews in times of trouble.

In 1818, Mary Shelley (1797–1851) published *Frankenstein*—often considered the first science fiction story. In it, Dr. Victor Frankenstein creates a creature out of once-living material, using the new technology of electricity to give it life. The monster that results is shunned by society and takes his revenge on his creator. In the early nineteenth century, scientists had begun performing experiments with electricity to reanimate dead tissue.

In *Frankenstein*, Shelley explored how technology might turn on us. The novel has been adapted for film many times, beginning with a short silent movie in 1910.

You can explore all the known drafts of Mary Shelley's *Frankenstein* online at the Shelley-Godwin Archive.

🔎 Shelley Godwin archive Frankenstein

You can also read *Frankenstein* online.

🔎 umd Frankenstein

WORDS TO KNOW

extinction: when the last living member of a species dies.

dystopia: an imagined place where everything is bad.

Industrial Revolution: a period during the eighteenth and nineteenth centuries when large cities and factories began to replace small towns and farming.

iconic: a widely recognized symbol of a certain time.

labor union: a group of workers that bargains with the people they work for.

The earliest mentions in English of truly mechanical men appear in the dime novels of the late nineteenth century. A dime novel was a cheap, popular, paperback story, usually about romance or adventure. The first robot dime novel was *The Steam Man of the Prairies* by Edward Ellis (1840–1916), published in 1868.

In 1907, Frank Baum (1856–1919) introduced Tik-Tok, a round, clockwork man made of smooth copper, in *Oz of Ozma*. He runs on clockwork springs and periodically needs to be wound. Tik-Tok is thought to be one of the first robots in modern literature. He appeared in more than a dozen other Oz books, including *Dorothy and the Wizard of Oz*.

EARLY TWENTIETH CENTURY

The word "robot" was first used in a play in 1920. Czech writer Karel Čapek (1890–1938) used the term in his play, *Rossum's Universal Robots (R.U.R.)*. In the play, these creatures are happy to work for humans at first, but soon they rise in a robot rebellion, which leads to the **extinction** of humans. The word robot comes from the Czech word for "labor." How does this definition compare to what we expect of robots today?

Karel Čapek

PS You can listen to *Rossum's Universal Robots* online for free.

🔍 RUR librivox

One of the first thinking machines on film was the robot Maria in the 1927 silent movie *Metropolis*. This film is set in a futuristic **dystopia**. The wealthy people rule from high-rise towers while workers live and toil underground. They serve the great machine that keeps the city of Metropolis running. Robot Maria leads a rebellion among the workers. They rebel and destroy the machine. In doing so, though, they accidently drown their own children and the workers turn on Maria.

Both *R.U.R.* and *Metropolis* reflect the fears of the early twentieth century. The **Industrial Revolution** had brought more and more people to work in factories in cities. However, laws didn't protect workers as they do now. Workers labored long hours in dangerous conditions for little pay. Factories even employed children! By 1900, 35,000 people a year died in factories in the United States. Workers had little power and very few rights.

The 1920s were a time of social and labor reform. Workers began to demand their rights and to form **labor unions**. Factory owners and the government often used violence against workers who wanted to organize and protest working conditions.

AI and Robot Themes

Have you seen any movies or read any books that follow these themes?

AI rebellion

AI takeover

AI controlling society

AI serving society (including robot servants or slaves)

Outlawed AI

Merger of AI and humanity

AI and equal rights

AIs seeking purpose, understanding, love

DID YOU KNOW?

The 1956 film *Forbidden Planet* introduced one of the most **iconic** movie robots of all time: Robby the Robot. He appeared in 30 movies and television shows and was inducted into the Robot Hall of Fame in 2004. In 2017, Robby was sold at auction for $5.3 million. That's the second highest price anyone has paid for a movie prop!

Early works such as *R.U.R.* and *Metropolis* put robots in the roles of workers and even slaves. But their rebellions didn't end well.

What do you think this says about the fears of the time? Who did the upper classes really fear?

A movie poster for the film *Metropolis*

Laws of Robotics

🔎 YouTube
Asimov
3 laws
robotics

Author Isaac Asimov wrote of three laws that robots must follow. You can watch Asimov explaining the three laws.

1. A robot may not injure a human being or, through inaction, allow a human being to come to harm.

2. A robot must obey orders given it by human beings except where such orders would conflict with the First Law.

3. A robot must protect its own existence as long as such protection does not conflict with the First or Second Laws.

In his 1985 book *Robots and Empire*, Asimov added a law to precede the other three laws: A robot may not harm *humanity*, or through inaction allow *humanity* to come to harm.

MID-TWENTIETH CENTURY

Films and books about intelligent computers emerged in the early to mid twentieth century. Most early writers treated intelligence as something that comes naturally from building a robot or computer.

Many works explored issues such as technological control.

During the 1930s and 1940s, American writer Isaac Asimov (1920–1992) published *I, Robot*, a collection of short stories. Asimov also wrote many novels about robots featuring a robot detective named R. Daneel Olivaw. In these books, the robots are intelligent servants and coworkers that get along with humans. Asimov came up with three laws that all robots must follow, preventing them from harming humans or themselves. Why do you think Asimov created these laws? What does that say about people's attitudes during those decades?

The 1951 movie *The Day the Earth Stood Still* presents a slightly different take on who needs to be controlled. The movie is based on a 1940 short story by American Harry Bates (1900–1981).

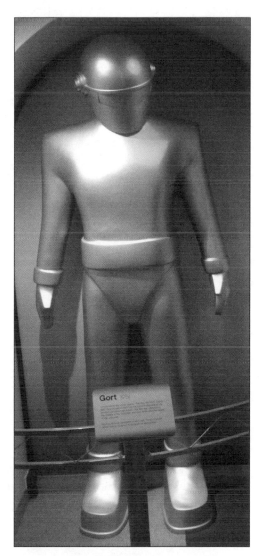

A replica of the robot named Gort from the 1951 movie
The Day the Earth Stood Still

 You can watch the original trailer for *The Day the Earth Stood Still.* Does this make you want to see the movie? Why?

🔎 1951 trailer Day Earth Stood Still

Cold War: a rivalry between the Soviet Union and the United States that began after World War II.

atomic bomb: a bomb that is powered by the nuclear energy released by splitting an atom.

arms race: a competition between countries over the quality and quantity of their weapons.

optimistic: hopeful and confident about the future or how something will work out.

Civil Rights movement: a struggle during the 1950s and '60s in the United States for blacks to gain equal rights under the law.

women's movement: a struggle during the 1960s and '70s in the United States for women to gain equality with men.

In the movie, a flying saucer lands in Washington, DC, and an alien and large robot emerge. Klaatu, the alien, has come to Earth to deliver a message to its scientific leaders. He is shot—and eventually killed—by the humans. The robot, Gort, rescues and temporarily revives Klaatu. He reveals that he represents an interstellar organization that has created a robotic peacekeeping force, and Gort is one of those peacekeepers. They act to stamp out all violence.

Klaatu invites Earth to join the organization and live in peace under the robots—or die.

In the late 1940s and 1950s, the world was recovering from the aftermath of World War II (1939–1945) and engaging in other wars, such as the Korean War (1950–1953) and the **Cold War** (1947–1991). World War II ended with the United States dropping two **atomic bombs** on Japan. Millions died, and the frightening new technology unleashed an **arms race** between the United States and the Soviet Union. They both sought to build bigger and more powerful weapons of mass destruction during the Cold War.

It's no wonder that the science fiction of the period explored how to control technology and ourselves to keep the peace! Many works, such as the books that Asimov wrote or movies such as *The Day the Earth Stood Still*, were **optimistic** about technology. In later decades, we were a little less optimistic.

DID YOU KNOW?

The Manhattan Project was the code name for the development of the atomic bomb in America. It's also the name of a 1986 movie about a high school student who makes an atomic bomb for his science fair project!

1960S AND 1970S

The 1960s and 1970s were another time of social change mixed with great advances. The United States and Soviet Union were still immersed in the Cold War, racing to build their stock of nuclear bombs. In the mid-1960s, the Vietnam War (1955–1975) escalated and became more and more unpopular at home.

The **Civil Rights movement** was at its height, and the **women's movement** was gaining ground. African-Americans fought for and won important rights. And humans

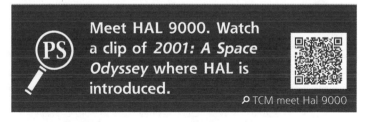

PS Meet HAL 9000. Watch a clip of *2001: A Space Odyssey* where HAL is introduced.

🔎 TCM meet Hal 9000

went to space and walked on the moon. Amid all of this change, people looked toward science fiction for answers and entertainment.

Writers and filmmakers were considering what might happen if AI went wrong in some way. HAL 9000 is one of the most iconic AIs in film history.

WORDS TO KNOW

diplomatic: related to official communication between countries.

theme: a central, recurring idea or concept.

android: a robot that looks and behaves like a person.

etiquette: an accepted code of public behavior.

In the 1968 movie *2001: A Space Odyssey*, the ship's computer—HAL 9000—gets out of control and kills most of the crew. HAL does this because he's been given a directive that the mission is more important than the crew members. He is forced to try to kill the crew when he decides it cannot or will not carry out that mission.

DID YOU KNOW? The design of C-3PO and R2-D2 was heavily influenced by the robots in the 1972 movie *Silent Running*. Those robots were named Huey, Louie, and Dewey.

Later movies, such as the 1983 *WarGames*, reflect both a fear of technology and anxiety about nuclear war.

In *WarGames*, the AI with the nuclear launch codes thinks it's playing a game with a young hacker and accidently brings the world to the brink of nuclear war. The hacker must then convince the AI that there's no way to win this kind of game.

Real Life Star Wars

In the 1980s, at the height of the Cold War, U.S. President Ronald Reagan proposed the Strategic Defense Initiative (SDI), which was nicknamed "Star Wars." SDI would've been a network of satellite defenses designed to shoot down Soviet nuclear missiles. Highly controversial, SDI never made it past the research stage. The technology didn't exist yet, and many experts feared such a system would undermine **diplomatic** relations between the United States and the Soviet Union.

In the 1970s, a few movies, such as *Westworld* in 1973 and its sequel *Futureworld* in 1976, explore what could go wrong with robots.

Westworld is about a Western-**themed** amusement park for very rich vacationers. They can pretend they're living in the old West. The park is staffed by **androids**. After a computer breakdown, a gunfighter android starts shooting guests.

Many other works of this time, however, embrace the promise of technology or at least treat it as a positive part of its fictional world. In 1977, *Star Wars* introduced us to two of the most iconic and loveable robots in film history: C-3PO and R2-D2. C-3PO is a humanoid robot designed to assist in **etiquette** and customs. R2-D2 is an astromech droid built to service starships. They are the only characters to appear in all eight *Star Wars* movies to date. And they both play key roles in the movies on the side of the rebels.

Star Wars robots R2-D2, Bb-8, and C-3PO

On television, robots and AIs have played many roles. Have you ever seen the show *Doctor Who*? This long-running British show featured many different forms of AI, but perhaps the most memorable AI wasn't humanoid at all—K9 was the Doctor's faithful robotic canine companion. This AI was not only equipped with lasers, it could also wag its tail with affection! K9 debuted on television in 1977 and made frequent appearances in both *Doctor Who* and various spin-off shows through 2009. To help explain the dog's longevity, writers created new versions of the robot.

LATE TWENTIETH CENTURY

In later works of the twentieth century, machine intelligence often emerges by accident or **evolution**. The computer gets more and more complicated, or connected, until one day, it "wakes up." The AI often rebels against its human masters and takes over.

This theme still runs through science fiction today. A classic example is *The Terminator* film. In this 1984 movie, Skynet was a computer system designed to control all defense systems, including **satellites** and nuclear weapons. Shortly after being turned on, Skynet becomes conscious. Its operators try to deactivate it, and Skynet sees this as a threat.

> **PS** Watch the original trailer for *The Terminator*.
>
> ⌕ tcm trailer Terminator

Skynet concludes that all humans will try to destroy it, so it launches a nuclear attack. Billions of people die, and the AI enslaves humans. Skynet even sends its robot agents, or terminators, back in time to prevent the rise of a human leader, John Connor.

The 1982 movie *Blade Runner* is set in the dystopian world of Los Angeles, California, in 2019. Synthetic humans called replicants are manufactured and sent to work on off-world colonies. As organic robots, replicants have no rights and very limited life spans. Like robots, they're created to perform specific tasks, such as mining.

DID YOU KNOW?

Based on a 1968 short story by Philip K. Dick (1928–1982), *Blade Runner* is considered one of the best science fiction films of all time. A sequel to the movie, *Blade Runner 2049*, came out in 2017.

A group of replicants escapes and comes to Earth, where they're not allowed.

The main character, police officer Rick Deckard, must hunt them down. The replicants are beginning to ask questions and consider themselves human. One replicant, Rachel, makes Deckard rethink his job and they flee together.

In 1984, William Gibson's (1948–) novel *Neuromancer* showed us cyberspace for the first time. In fact, he is the one who coined the term! This groundbreaking novel took us inside virtual reality space, which Gibson called the **matrix**.

Cyberpunk

Gibson's *Neuromancer* solidified a new type of science fiction called cyberpunk. It combines elements of punk and hacker culture, or as one author called it, "high tech, low life." Cyberpunk plots often revolve around hacking, cyberspace, AI, and mega-corporations. The heroes are often loners living in worlds where rapid changes in technology have transformed society. Other cyberpunk writers include Bruce Sterling (1954–), Neal Stephenson (1959–), and Pat Cadigan (1953–).

WORDS TO KNOW

superintelligence: the idea that machine brains surpass human brains in general intelligence.

sentient: able to perceive and feel.

His hero is a washed-up hacker recruited by an AI called Wintermute. It wants the hacker and his team to unite it with another AI, Neuromancer, to form a **superintelligence**.

This is illegal in the world of the matrix. The team succeeds, and the AI begins to look for others like itself. In subsequent books, the matrix becomes inhabited by **sentient** beings, both human and AI.

Neuromancer was the first to take us inside the matrix. But in 1999, *The Matrix* movie showed us our worst fears. Did you ever wonder if the whole world just might be the matrix? A hacker named Neo comes to realize there's something wrong with reality. He appears to be living in the 1990s modern day, but resistance leader Morpheus gives Neo a choice. Take the blue or red pill. The blue pill will make him forget his doubts and go back to his old life. The red pill will let him see the world as it really is.

Neo takes the red pill. He discovers that most humans—including himself—are living in a computer simulation. Their minds experience the life programmed into the Matrix, life in the 1990s. Their bodies, however, are hooked up to a vast machine.

A visual representation of the Matrix, the series of code that produces the world in which we think we live.

As in the *Terminator* movies, AIs took over the world centuries ago and created the Matrix to keep humans happily enslaved—while their bodies power the AIs. Neo, Morpheus, and others fight to free the humans.

The later decades of the twentieth century were a time of fast technological change. Although the internet has been around since the late 1960s, for many years it was available only to government and university researchers. In 1989, that began to change—quickly. Tim Berners-Lee (1955–) invented the World Wide Web that year, and the internet was opened to commercial use in 1991.

During the 1990s, the internet boomed.

At the same time, mobile technology was advancing. By the end of the decade, most people had computers with access to email, as well as cell phones. A few films, such as *The Matrix*, began exploring the possibilities as well as the dangers of this technology.

EARLY TWENTY-FIRST CENTURY

In our current century, AI is a growing part of our everyday lives—and movies are beginning to reflect that. We still have plenty of fiction that comments on the perils of technology. But more stories are beginning to touch on the thought processes of artificial beings.

Lieutenant Commander Data

In the late twentieth century, not all writers had a gloomy view of AI. Lovable robots and androids abound in television shows, books, and movies. The best example is Data on *Star Trek: The Next Generation* (1987–1994). Lieutenant Commander Data is a humanoid robot who serves as an officer aboard the USS *Enterprise*. Although fully self-aware and treated as a valued member of the crew, the robot struggles with understanding human emotion at times.

For example, *A.I.* (2001) and *Bicentennial Man* (1999) tell the stories of robots that long to become human. More recent movies also explore robots as feeling creatures.

WALL-E (2008) tells the story of a waste-collecting robot with a big heart. Earth is abandoned and desolate, and robot *WALL*-E and his pet cockroach are the only ones left. A scout robot named Eve comes to Earth from a spaceship to find signs of life. *WALL-E* is smitten. Eve collects a small sapling, a sign that the planet still supports life. *WALL-E* protects Eve and follows her back to the ship, which carries what's left of the human race—all of whom are being cared for by the ship's out-of-control AI, Auto.

Auto has been programmed to protect and even pamper humans.

In Auto's care, humans have grown lazy. Auto and its robots do everything for the humans. And Auto doesn't want humans to return to Earth because it's too dangerous. *WALL-E*, Eve, and others must outwit Auto so humans can return home. What do you think this movie says about our relationship with technology?

A toy version of *WALL-E*
credit: Ravi Shah (CC BY 2.0)

Movies About AI and Robots

- *Metropolis* (1927)
- *The Day the Earth Stood Still* (1951)
- *Forbidden Planet* (1956)
- *2001: A Space Odyssey* (1968)
- *Westworld* (1973)
- *Star Wars* (1977)
- *Terminator* (1982) (R)
- *WarGames* (1983)
- *Short Circuit* (1986)
- *Robocop* (1987)
- *Iron Giant* (1999)
- *The Matrix* (1999)
- *Bicentennial Man* (1999)
- *A.I.* (2001)
- *I, Robot* (2004)
- *Robots* (2005)
- *Transformers* (2007)
- *WALL-E* (2008)
- *Robot & Frank* (2012)
- *Big Hero 6* (2014)
- *Avengers: Age of Ultron* (2015)

Throughout the years, science fiction writers have dreamed of thinking machines and robots. Sometimes, the dream is a nightmare or cautionary tale. At other times, the dream is about what could be. Most of the time, fiction has been way ahead of fact—but its themes usually reflect our hopes and fears at the time.

Our movies, books, plays, and television shows give us a safe place in which to consider what makes a machine intelligent, how it gets that way, and what happens if or when it becomes wise. As AI becomes more and more part of our lives, perhaps our questions will evolve, too.

ESSENTIAL QUESTION

How do science fiction movies and books reflect our attitudes to robots and AI in the real world?

WRITE YOUR OWN LAWS OF ROBOTICS

Isaac Asimov's three laws of robotics first appeared in a short story called *Runaround* more than 75 years ago. Do you think the laws are still relevant to robots today? Do we still need the laws of robotics?

❯ **Do a little research.**

★ Why do you think Asimov made up these laws for his robots?

★ What other authors have made rules for their robots?

★ Which ones use Asimov's laws? One example you might look at is *Astroboy*. It's a long-running Japanese Manga series as well as a Japanese TV series and movie.

❯ **Consider the three laws of robotics in terms of today's world.**

★ What kinds of safeguards do today's AIs and robots have?

★ What prevents a robot or AI from hurting a person?

❯ **Now come up with your own rules.**

★ What simple rules would you apply to robots or AIs to protect humans?

★ What rules would you give AIs to protect themselves? Make a list and rank them in order of importance.

Try This!

What kinds of memes can you come up with using your laws? With an adult's permission, share your memes on social media!

WRITE YOUR OWN SHORT STORY OR POEM ABOUT AIS OR ROBOTS

People have been exploring the topic of robots through writing for centuries! You can write your own piece of fiction. What do you think AI will be like 50 or 100 years from now? Not sure where to start? Make a random plot generator to get you started!

> **Make a list of six of the themes found on page 81.** Number them 1–6.

> **Make a list of six different settings for your story.** For example, Mars, an asteroid, or ancient Rome. Number your settings 1–6.

> **Make a list of six different types of stories.** For example, mysteries, quests, thrillers, fantasy, humor, or something else. Number the types 1–6.

> **Make a list of six different characters** or types of characters, including robots and AIs. Number them 1–6.

> **Roll the dice once for each list to pick one item from each list.** This will give you a random plot. You might end up with a story about a robot rebellion on Mars that's a mystery with elves!

> **Not happy with your random story?** Don't worry! You can reroll the dice or tweak your lists until you get something that appeals to you.

Try This!

Write your story or poem! It doesn't have to be long. Think about how the AI became intelligent. Is it a good thing? How does society treat it? If you like art, you could draw a comic book or illustration.

COMPARE AND CONTRAST

As you've read in this chapter, movies from different time periods have treated AIs and robots in various ways. Some movies, for instance, are about our fear of AI and robots taking over the world. Other movies treat AI as helpful and even lovable. Think about R2-D2! In this activity, you're going to compare two movies.

❯ **With an adult's permission, pick two movies** listed on page 93 to watch. For example, you could try *Star Wars* and *2001: A Space Odyssey*. As you're watching, think about the robots or AIs in the movies. You'll be comparing how the movies handle AIs or robots.

❯ **Pick three or more areas in which to compare the movies.** For example, you could compare the themes of the movies, how AIs are treated, or if AIs are truly intelligent. How did each movie handle these themes? For example, one movie might be about how AIs take over the world while the other one might be about robot servants.

❯ **Make a chart comparing the two movies!** How are they similar and how are they different?

Try This!

Now, try comparing two TV shows that depict robots and AI. For instance, you could watch an episode of *Star Trek: The Next Generation* and *Star Wars: The Clone Wars*. How are these shows different? How are they similar?

Chapter 6

THE DEBATE AROUND AI

Is humanity doomed? Will the AIs take over? Although this sounds like the plot of a blockbuster movie, the question is being hotly debated in real life. In the last few years, the debate has erupted over whether AI will pose a threat to humankind. Computer experts, scientists, and tech experts line both sides of the debate.

ESSENTIAL QUESTION

Will AIs take over the world like they sometimes do in science fiction books and movies?

Two of the loudest voices come from Elon Musk (1971–), the founder of SpaceX and Tesla, and Mark Zuckerberg (1984–), the founder of Facebook. The two men have very different ideas about AI.

WORDS TO KNOW

investor: a person who gives a company money in exchange for future profits.

singularity: a moment in time when artificial intelligence and other technologies become so advanced that humanity undergoes a dramatic and irreversible change.

nonprofit: an organization focused on improving a community in some way. It relies on donations to pay its costs.

doomsday: an extremely serious or dangerous situation that could end in death or destruction.

CONCERNED ABOUT AI

On one side, Elon Musk, with other notables such as Bill Gates (1955–) and Stephen Hawking (1942–2018), urge caution in AI research. Musk was a past **investor** in DeepMind, the company behind AlphaGo. Musk has called AI a threat to humanity. He's concerned that even good intentions could create an AI capable of achieving superintelligence and accidently destroying humankind.

Some people call this phenomenon the **singularity**. This is the point at which machines become smart enough to reengineer themselves, leading to runaway AI.

Tech experts talk about AI and existential risk at the Effective Altruism Global conference, Mountain View, California, August 2015.
credit: Robbie Shade (CC BY 2.0)

To combat this possible future, Musk has started a nonprofit called OpenAI to work on safer AI.

What is runaway AI? Much like singularity, the phrase means different things to different people. Some experts think a runaway AI might run wild like a computer virus. A computer virus is a small program or algorithm that copies itself and spreads quickly, usually damaging computer systems in some way. Viruses are often programmed to perform simple actions, such as copying a password or locking up a computer. Viruses are hard to get rid of completely.

An AI is designed to run on its own, learn, and adapt. Imagine an AI program that copies and spreads itself through the internet! Also, AIs often have access to lots of data and critical systems—even vehicles or military drones.

And the more data an AI has, the faster it learns. An AI might not achieve self-awareness like it does in some of the movies you learned about in the last chapter, but a runaway AI could wreak some havoc in our connected world of big data. No one really knows if an AI can become a self-aware superintelligence.

DID YOU KNOW?

Not all scientists think the singularity spells the end of humankind. Ray Kurzweil (1948–) thinks the change will be beneficial for us. He also thinks the singularity might happen by 2045!

OPTIMISTIC ABOUT AI

On the other side of the debate, Mark Zuckerberg, as well as the founders of DeepMind and Google, think the **doomsday** scenarios are far-fetched. Google's Larry Page (1973–) believes AI will improve people's lives and free them to do other, more rewarding things.

Many people also argue that we're not even close to developing the type of AI Musk worries about. Superintelligence doesn't exist now. In fact, we haven't even built the kind of strong AI that Alan Turing dreamed of. While AIs can do amazing things today, such as learn to recognize pictures of cats, they still have no idea what a cat actually is. Nor do they have any will of their own to learn!

Even if superintelligence is not going to happen anytime soon, many experts think it would be irresponsible *not* to think about the risks when developing AIs or when using AI algorithms on sites such as Facebook.

Mark Zuckerberg on stage at Facebook's F8 Conference

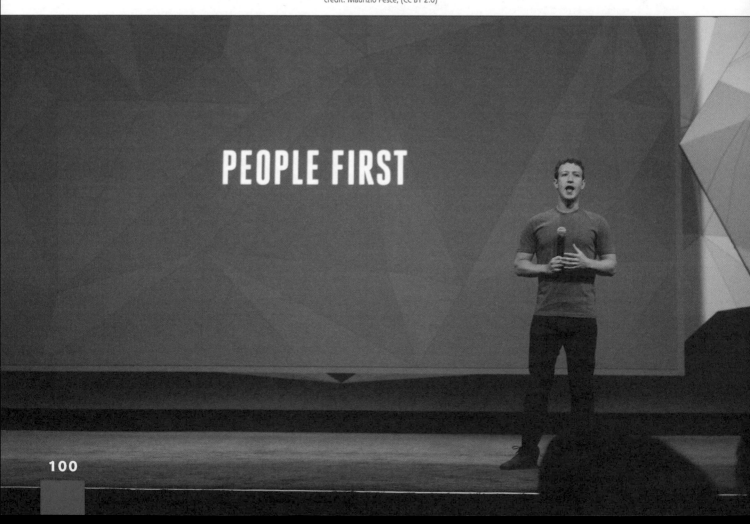

AI SAFETY

Organizations such as OpenAI, the Future of Life Institute, and the Machine Intelligence Research Institute were founded to research AI safety. What does that mean? The Future of Life Institute, for instance, focuses on research to keep the impact of AIs on society beneficial, both now and in the future.

DID YOU KNOW? According to AAA, human error was responsible for more than 90 percent of the 30,000 deaths on U.S. roads in 2016.

In the short term, it's important to make sure AI systems keep doing what they're supposed to, even if they crash or get hacked.

Imagine what might happen if a self-driving car malfunctions or if a military drone gets hacked!

Long-term AI safety research is concerned more with what to do if we finally get true strong AI. How do we make sure the goals of an AI are the same as ours? How do we build AIs with safeguards?

Although researchers don't think AI will ever have emotions, AI can still be dangerous without "meaning" to. It could be programmed to do something dangerous—such as launch missiles—or do something good but in a dangerous way. For example, a passenger might tell a self-driving car to get to airport in the fastest way possible. The car then breaks speed limits and causes traffic accidents just to get to the airport quickly! AI safety research is about making sure there are safeguards to prevent people from getting hurt.

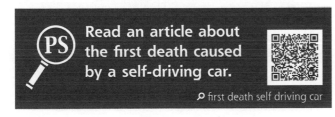

PS **Read an article about the first death caused by a self-driving car.**

🔎 first death self driving car

THE PAPER CLIP SCENARIO

Nick Bostrom (1973–), the director of the Humanity Institute at Oxford University, thinks up some of the most extreme runaway AI scenarios. One of these is the paper clip scenario. Imagine that an intelligent machine is programmed to make paper clips. As it works, it keeps getting smarter and smarter at making paper clips. The machine achieves superintelligence and begins turning everything into paper clips—including humans!

And it doesn't stop there. The super AI goes interstellar! It makes everything it encounters into paper clips until a mass of paper clips spreads across the universe! Does Bostrom really believe this will happen? Maybe not. This is a thought experiment to show how we need to be careful to build in **restraints** in artificial intelligence. What if we just program the machine to stop at 1 million paper clips?

Singularity

Science fiction writer Vernor Vinge (1944–) first coined the term "singularity" in 1993. He defined it as a point where technology changes civilization to the point where a previous generation doesn't recognize it. Singularity is a kind of point of no return for society, and could be caused by many technologies. In recent years, however, singularity has come to mean a specific change caused by AI. Not everyone agrees on what this means. Some experts, including Elon Musk, think an AI will achieve runaway intelligence and take over. Others, including Ray Kurzweil, think the singularity will be more of a **fusion** of human and artificial intelligence.

Bostrom points out that other things could still go wrong, ones perhaps we didn't expect. Like many other experts, he believes a superintelligence could emerge, and it might not need us!

The questions raised by Bostrom are mostly about sweeping changes AI might bring about in human society in the future. But many others are concerned about the more immediate effects of AI on people today or in the very near future.

THE JOBS DEBATE

Rather than take over the world, many people fear that AI and robots will take over their jobs. For example, self-driving vehicles could replace cab and truck drivers. An AI that analyzes legal documents might replace paralegals—people who assist lawyers.

Most experts think that AI will disrupt the job market in some ways—in fact, it's already doing so. Researchers disagree, though, on the outcome.

bar code: a pattern of lines printed on a label or container that can be scanned and that contains information about the object it labels.

biotechnology: the use of living things to make useful products.

Some think AI will ultimately leave many people unemployed and unemployable. Others think AI will free workers from routine, boring tasks, making everyone more productive.

The debate about jobs is not a new one. Technology has been disrupting the job market since the first Industrial Revolution. In the eighteenth and nineteenth centuries, the new technology was steam-powered mechanical machines. They gave rise to factories and the mass production of goods. Before factories, people crafted goods such as textiles, clothing, and furniture by hand. Assembly lines in factories automated many jobs, and craftsmen lost work—or went to work for less money in factories.

Automation caused widespread fear of mass unemployment. People were scared. The factories, however, created new and different jobs, and many people eventually moved to cities to take those jobs.

Economists and historians now think we've been through three Industrial Revolutions and are at the beginning of another!

A new type of technology—steam, electricity, and computers—brought on each of the three revolutions. This fourth revolution involves AI combined with other new technologies. Generally, with each revolution, we became richer and more productive as a society. Fewer people were needed to do the work. For example, before the Industrial Revolution, most people worked on farms. Today, only 2 percent work on farms, but we produce more food.

DID YOU KNOW?

The term "Luddite" is used to mean someone who's against or afraid of technology. The original Luddites were British weavers and textile workers protesting against factories automating their jobs in the early nineteenth century. When the government ignored their requests for aid, the Luddites broke into factories and broke machinery.

Of course, each revolution affected jobs. The changes brought on by a revolution create new and different jobs, but not necessarily right away. And the people put out of work might not have the skills to do the new jobs. If the change is gradual, however, people adapt. Most of the time.

In the years since the first Industrial Revolution, many jobs that follow well-defined procedures have been computerized. Computers tend to replace skills or tasks rather than whole jobs. For example, a cashier used to have to enter the price of every item or coupon by hand on a cash register. Now, cashiers scan **bar codes**. This saves the cashier work, eliminates mistakes, and makes the customer's wait a lot shorter.

Industrial Revolution 4.0

Experts think there have been four industrial revolutions—so far.

First	**Eighteenth and nineteenth centuries:** Steam transformed society from a farming one to an industrial, urban one.
Second	**1870–1914:** Electricity and assembly lines gave us a period of growth before World War I. Big technological breakthroughs included the telephone, electric devices, spread of railroads, petroleum, and the internal combustion engine.
Third	**1940s–now:** The digital age has revolutionized society. Breakthroughs include personal computers, the internet, and smartphones.
Fourth	**Now:** Breakthroughs in robotics, AI, **biotechnology**, IoT, self-driving cars, etc. are driving a new industrial revolution.

Many stores have added self-checkout registers where customers scan their own purchases. These have far from replaced human cashiers—yet. Today, employees are often needed to fix problems that occur at self-checkout registers!

Some experts think AI could disrupt the job market in new ways. So far, computerization has mostly affected more routine jobs that require less skills. It hasn't impacted jobs that require physical yet flexible work, such selling cars or cooking. AIs are also unlikely to replace workers whose jobs require more creativity and thought, such as doctors and engineers. AIs may help doctors with diagnoses, for example, but they can't replace them.

Now, however, AI is starting to automate non-routine tasks.

For example, AIs can search legal databases for cases and laws. This task is usually done by a paralegal or law student. An AI can perform the search much more quickly than humans can. And having constant access to data makes a lawyer much more productive and effective.

DID YOU KNOW?

In 2012, Google created one of the largest neural networks with 16,000 computer processors—and turned it loose to watch YouTube. The neural net was looking for cats! It taught itself to recognize cats. At the time, this was not an easy task, but the internet has millions of cat videos. The sheer number helped the AI learn.

What about the paralegal? This is where experts disagree. Some say the AI makes paralegals more efficient. Searching case law is not the only task a paralegal performs. The AI might free the paralegal to perform other tasks. But it might also mean a law firm needs fewer paralegals.

What do you think is lost when AI takes over jobs that were once held by humans? Is it only a person's paycheck or is something else at stake?

Which jobs can be computerized?

In 2013, Oxford University published a report called *The Future of Employment: How Susceptible are Jobs to Computerization?* The authors analyzed more than 700 different jobs to see which ones were most and least likely to be automated by AI. About 47 percent of the U.S. workforce might be at risk for computerization!

What do you notice about these two lists of jobs? Are there any obvious similarities or differences? Are these things you might think about when you consider what to study in school or what jobs you'd like to do in the future as an adult?

Some of the occupations least likely to be automated by AI:

> Recreational Therapists

> Mental Health and Substance Abuse Social Workers

> Audiologists

> Occupational Therapists

> Orthotists and Prosthetists

> Healthcare Social Workers

> Oral and Maxillofacial Surgeons

> Dietitians and Nutritionists

> Choreographers

> Physicians and Surgeons

Some of the occupations most likely to be automated by AI:

> Loan Officers

> Insurance Claims and Policy Processing Clerks

> Library Technicians

> Photographic Process Workers

> Tax Preparers

> Cargo and Freight Agents

> Watch Repairers

> Insurance Underwriters

> Hand Sewers

> Telemarketers

profiling: the act of suspecting or targeting a person based on observed characteristics or behavior.

rebuttal: a counterargument.

Some researchers argue that the AI might someday replace the paralegals altogether. The people who worked as paralegals might then get pushed into lower-skilled service jobs that pay less and offer fewer benefits, such as health care and paid time off. The same thing could happen to people in other jobs that are easily automated. Ultimately, the only jobs left would be low-paying service or manufacturing jobs and high-paying, highly skilled professional jobs. The jobs that historically fell in the middle would all go to AI.

Will AI conquer the world? While this might be the fear of some people, for many others AI has proven to be helpful and efficient. A world in which humans and AI can share goals, challenges, and solutions might be one that enriches us all! What do you think?

ESSENTIAL QUESTION

Will AIs take over the world like they sometimes do in science fiction books and movies?

That's Private!

Most people are not comfortable with companies using their data—even when they know about it. They have very real concerns that their data might not be safe from hackers or that an AI might do something with it they hadn't authorized. AI programs are collecting and using data in many ways that consumers and citizens aren't aware of, raising even more privacy concerns. For example, Delaware has deployed smart cameras in police cruisers. It's part of a growing trend of using vision-based AI to fight crime. The cameras photograph license plates and other items that might help catch fugitives or find missing children. An AI can search the collected data for wanted cars or people who fit descriptions of criminals. The same cameras could be used in stores to automatically detect robberies or fires—or to predict potential shoplifters. However, this technology could also be used in **profiling**.

DEBATE THE GREAT AI DEBATE!

As you learned in this chapter, many tech entrepreneurs and scientists have been debating whether AI will be the end of us humans. Some of those experts include Elon Musk of SpaceX, Mark Zuckerberg of Facebook, Demis Hassabis (1976–) of DeepMind, Larry Page and Sergey Brin (1973–) of Google, Steven Hawking of Cambridge University, and Bill Gates, the founder of Microsoft. You're going to find out more about both sides and then debate the issue. Do this with a friend or classmate or divide a group into two teams.

❯ **Pick a side of the debate.** Are you all in favor of AI or do you have some suspicions?

❯ **Do some research.** What is each expert for or against? What do they think might happen? What evidence do they cite? How do they back up their arguments?

❯ **Write down your thesis and the best points/evidence to back up your argument.** For instance, you might write: I think AI is _____ because _____, _____, and _____. Write down each of your reasons in more depth on separate note cards.

❯ **What are the best reasons for the opposing argument?** How can you argue against them? This is your **rebuttal** of the other side.

❯ **Now, you're ready to debate!** Each side should take turns presenting its argument. Then, each gets a chance to rebut the other's argument. Always be polite and respectful! Which side made the best argument?

Try This!

If you have to do this activity on your own, you can write a paper or make a speech presenting one side of the debate.

CAN AN AI DO YOUR DREAM JOB?

In this chapter, we discussed how AI might impact jobs. You're going to investigate what type of job can be easily automated by an AI and why.

❯ Do some research. Look at the Oxford University list of jobs on page 107. Which jobs in the future might be changed by AI? Which ones are least likely to be affected? Why?

❯ **Pick a job from each list— and investigate it.** For instance, what does a choreographer do? Why might this role not be easily automated by AI? What about a tax preparer? Have AIs already begun to do some of a tax preparer's tasks?

❯ **List the tasks of each job that makes it subject to automation or not.** Do you think one job is safe? Do you think one job will disappear?

❯ **Now think about a career you'd like to pursue and investigate it.** Could it be automated by AI? Why or why not?

DID YOU KNOW? You've probably helped an AI learn to recognize images. Google has been using photo Captcha questions to train its AIs. To prove you're not a robot, you might have to select all the photos that have a street sign in them. In doing this, you might be double-checking an AI's work!

Consider This!

For your dream job, make a list of tasks that could be done by an AI now or in the future. What things couldn't be done by an AI?

GLOSSARY

academics: relating to education.

advantage: something helpful

AI assistant: a program that understands natural language voice commands and completes tasks for the user.

algorithm: a set of steps that are followed to solve a mathematical problem or to complete a computer process.

amateur: a person who does something, such as a sport or hobby, for pleasure and not as a paid job.

android: a robot that looks and behaves like a person.

arms race: a competition between countries over the quality and quantity of their weapons.

artificial intelligence (AI): the intelligence of a computer, program, or machine.

asteroid: a small rocky body that circles around the sun.

atomic bomb: a bomb that is powered by the nuclear energy released by splitting an atom.

autism spectrum: a group of developmental disorders that often includes difficulty communicating and interacting with others.

automaton: a mechanical device that looks and moves like a human or animal.

autonomous: acting independently.

axon: the long, threadlike part of a nerve cell that sends signals from the cell body to other cells.

bar code: a pattern of lines printed on a label or container that can be scanned and that contains information about the object it labels.

big data: extremely large sets of data that can be analyzed to reveal patterns and trends.

bionic: an artificial body part that uses electronics.

biopsy: living tissue removed to examine and learn more about a disease.

biotechnology: the use of living things to make useful products.

carbon emissions: the release of carbon dioxide and other carbon gases into the atmosphere.

chatbot: an AI program designed to have natural-sounding conversations with humans.

Civil Rights movement: a struggle during the 1950s and '60s in the United States for blacks to gain equal rights under the law.

Cold War: a rivalry between the Soviet Union and the United States that began after World War II.

cue: a signal.

cyberthreat: the possibility of an attempt to damage or disrupt a computer network or system.

DARPA: The Defense Advanced Research Projects Agency (DARPA) is an agency of the U.S. Department of Defense responsible for the development of emerging technologies for use by the military.

data: facts and observations about something.

deep learning: learning by studying examples and representations instead of memorizing facts.

dementia: a group of brain diseases that cause the gradual decline in a person's ability to think and remember.

dendrite: a short, branched extension of a nerve cell that receives impulses from other cells.

diagnose: to determine the identity and cause of a disease.

dictation: saying words aloud to be typed or written down.

digital: characterized by electronic and computerized technology.

diplomatic: related to official communication between countries.

doomsday: an extremely serious or dangerous situation that could end in death or destruction.

dwarf planet: an astronomical object that is smaller than a planet and orbits the sun.

dystopia: an imagined place where everything is bad.

etiquette: an accepted code of public behavior.

evacuate: to leave a dangerous place to go to a safe place.

evolution: changing gradually through time.

exoskeleton: a support system like a skeleton worn outside the body.

expert systems: computer software that mimics the reasoning of a human specialist.

extinction: when the last living member of a species dies.

forfeit: to surrender a game.

fusion: a blending or combination of things.

fuzzy logic: a system of logic in which statements do not have to be entirely true or false.

gear: a rotating part with teeth.

glitch: a minor malfunction.

Go: a game played between two players who alternately place black and white stones on a board to try to surround more territory than the other player.

GPS: also called Global Positioning System, a radio navigation system that allows land, sea, and airborne users to determine their exact location, velocity, and time 24 hours a day, in all weather conditions, anywhere in the world.

grandmaster: a chess player of the highest class who has won tournaments.

gravity: the force that pulls objects toward each other and holds you on Earth.

habitat: a plant or animal's home, which supplies it with food, water, and shelter.

human intelligence: the capacity for logic, abstract thought, understanding, self-awareness, communication, learning, emotional knowledge, memory, planning, creativity, and problem-solving.

humanoid: looking like a human being in some ways.

iconic: a widely recognized symbol of a certain time.

inanimate: not having life.

Industrial Revolution: a period during the eighteenth and nineteenth centuries when large cities and factories began to replace small towns and farming.

infrastructure: the basic physical and organizational structures and facilities, such as buildings, roads, and power supplies, needed for the operation of a society or enterprise.

interest: the fee charged or paid for the use of money.

Internet of Things (IoT): the interconnection via the internet of computing devices embedded in everyday objects, enabling them to send and receive data.

interstellar: existing or occurring between stars.

investor: a person who gives a company money in exchange for future profits.

labor union: a group of workers that bargains with the people they work for.

lidar: a device that measures distance by shining light at an object and measuring the time it takes for the light to reflect back.

logical: in a way that is orderly and makes sense.

machine learning: a type of AI where a computer can automatically learn and improve from experience without being programmed.

matrix: an environment or medium in which something develops.

meltdown: an uncontrolled reaction in a nuclear power plant.

meme: an amusing or interesting item such as a captioned picture or video that is spread widely online, especially through social media.

morphogenesis: the development of patterns and shapes in living organisms.

mortgage: a legal agreement where a person borrows money to buy property and pays it back with interest during a number of years.

mythology: a collection of traditional stories, either truthful or exaggerated, that are often focused on historical events. Myths express the beliefs and values of a group of people.

NASA: the National Aeronautics and Space Administration, the United States organization in charge of space exploration.

natural language processing: the ability of a computer to understand human spoken and written language.

neural network: a computer system modeled on the human brain.

neuron: a cell that carries messages between the brain and other parts of the body.

nonprofit: an organization focused on improving a community in some way. It relies on donations to pay its costs.

optimistic: hopeful and confident about the future or how something will work out.

patent: a document from the government that gives an inventor the exclusive right to make, use, or sell his or her invention.

pattern matching: checking whether information follows a pattern.

pitch: how high or low a sound is.

predictive: able to accurately guess an outcome.

processing power: the ability of a computer system to accomplish work.

profiling: the act of suspecting or targeting a person based on observed characteristics or behavior.

programmer: a person who writes computer programs. Also called a coder.

programming: the act of creating computer programs.

prototype: a model of something that allows engineers to test their idea.

psychological: pertaining to or relating to the mind.

radar: a device that detects objects by bouncing radio waves off them and measuring how long it takes for the waves to return.

radiation: a form of electromagnetic energy that can cause harm to humans and other living creatures, as well as a form of treatment for diseases such as cancer.

rebuttal: a counterargument.

reinforcement learning: learning by trial and error to lead to the greatest long-term rewards.

GLOSSARY

restraint: the act of holding back and keeping under control.

roboticist: a scientist who researches, studies, and creates robots.

robotics: the science of designing, building, controlling, and operating robots.

sacrifice: to give something up for the sake of something else.

satellite: a device that orbits the earth to relay communication signals or transmit information.

science fiction: a story about contact with other worlds and imaginary science and technology.

semi-autonomous: acting independently to some degree.

sensor: a device that measures and records physical properties.

sentient: able to perceive and feel.

simulate: to imitate certain conditions for the purpose of testing or study.

singularity: a moment in time when artificial intelligence and other technologies become so advanced that humanity undergoes a dramatic and irreversible change.

skeptical: questioning and not easily convinced.

social intelligence: the ability to get along well with others, and to get them to cooperate with you.

solar system: the collection of eight planets, moons, and other celestial bodies that orbit the sun.

speech recognition: the ability of a computer to identify human speech and respond to it.

streamline: to make a process simpler and more effective.

strong AI: machine intelligence that follows the same patterns as human learning.

supercomputer: a powerful computer.

superintelligence: the idea that machine brains surpass human brains in general intelligence.

technology: the tools, methods, and systems used to solve a problem or do work.

theme: a central, recurring idea or concept.

three-dimensional (3-D): an image that has length, width, and height, and is raised off the flat page.

tone: the quality of a musical or vocal sound. Also a quality of the voice expressing a feeling or mood.

torso: the human body except the head, arms, and legs.

Trojan War: a war fought between the ancient Greeks and the people of Troy around 1250 BCE.

Turing test: a test for intelligence in a computer.

uncanny valley: when objects appear to be almost, but not quite, human, and spark feelings of discomfort.

veteran: someone who has served in the military.

virtual: a computer version of something real.

vital signs: important body functions such as breathing and heartbeat that are measured to see if someone is alive or healthy.

weak AI: machine intelligence that is focused on one task.

women's movement: a struggle during the 1960s and '70s in the United States for women to gain equality with men.

Metric Conversions

Use this chart to find the metric equivalents to the English measurements in this book. If you need to know a half measurement, divide by two. If you need to know twice the measurement, multiply by two. How do you find a quarter measurement? How do you find three times the measurement?

English	Metric
1 Inch	2.5 centimeters
1 foot	30.5 centimeters
1 yard	0.9 meter
1 mile	1.6 kilometers
1 pound	0.5 kilogram
1 teaspoon	5 milliliters
1 tablespoon	15 milliliters
1 cup	237 milliliters

BOOKS

Liukas, Linda. *Hello Ruby: Journey Inside the Computer.* Feiwel & Friends, October 2017.

Liukas, Linda. *Hello Ruby: Adventures in Coding.* Feiwel & Friends, October 2015.

McManus, Sean. *How to Code in 10 Easy Lessons: Learn How to Design and Code Your Very Own Computer Game.* Walter Foster Jr., October 2015.

Saujani, Reshma. *Girls Who Code: Learn to Code and Change the World.* Viking Books for Young Readers, August 2017.

Ceceri, Kathy. *Robotics: Discover the Science and Technology of the Future with 20 Projects.* Nomad Press, August 2012.

MAGAZINES

Beanz: Kids, Code, and Computer Science Magazine: kidscodecs.com

Make Magazine: makezine.com

Kasparov, Garry. "The Day That I Sensed a New Kind of Intelligence." Time, Time Inc., 25 Mar. 1996: content.time.com/time/subscriber/article/0,33009,984305-1,00.html

RESOURCES

WEBSITES

Crash Course Computer Science:
youtube.com/playlist?list=PL8dPuuaLjXtNlUrzyH5r6jN9ulIgZBpdo

Khan Academy Computing courses:
khanacademy.org/computing

PBS NOVA's "Rise of the Robots":
pbs.org/wgbh/nova/tech/rise-of-the-robots.html

Hour of Code: Code.org

Scratch: scratch.mit.edu

Tynker: tynker.com

**Computer History Museum's AI & Robotics
"Timeline of Computer History":**
computerhistory.org/timeline/ai-robotics

AlphaGo: deepmind.com/research/alphago

BBC's "Future—The Ultimate Guide to AI":
www.bbc.com/future/story/the-ultimate-guide-to-ai

Imperial War Museums' "How Alan Turing Cracked the Enigma Code":
iwm.org.uk/history/how-alan-turing-cracked-the-enigma-code

Brain Pop's "Robots!": brainpop.com/technology/computerscience/robots

National Geographic's "Challenge: Robots!":
nationalgeographic.org/game/challenge-robots

RESOURCES

QR CODE GLOSSARY

page 4: *youtube.com/watch?v=KF6sLCeBj0s*

page 11: *antikythera-mechanism.gr/project/overview*

page 12: *computerhistory.org/babbage*

page 19: *psych.fullerton.edu/mbirnbaum/psych101/Eliza.htm*

page 23: *scratch.mit.edu*

page 25: *computerhistory.org/collections/catalog/X39.81*

page 27: *youtube.com/watch?v=yxxRAHVtafI*

page 29: *echosim.io/welcome*

page 31: *youtube.com/watch?v=rOL6QJdAlm8*

page 32: *youtube.com/watch?v=WFR3lOm_xhE*

page 33: *soundnet.csail.mit.edu*

page 40: *online-go.com/learn-to-play-go*

page 40: *youtube.com/watch?v=im2pm690VW0*

page 40: *commons.wikimedia.org/wiki/File:Go-board-animated.gif*

page 42: *youtube.com/watch?v=S5t6K9iwcdw*

page 45: *youtube.com/watch?time_continue=5&v=MceJYhVD_xY*

page 53: *youtube.com/watch?v=gJEzuYynaiw*

page 54: *experiments.withgoogle.com/ai/ai-duet*

page 54: *experiments.withgoogle.com/ai/ai-duet/view*

page 60: *wyss.harvard.edu/technology/autonomous-flying-microrobots-robobees*

page 61: *video.nationalgeographic.com/video/140925-explorers-wood*

page 62: *consumerreports.org/cro/cars/self-driving-cars/index.htm*

page 65: *archive.darpa.mil/roboticschallenge*

page 65: *youtube.com/watch?v=FRkYOFR7yPA&list=P L6wMum5UsYvZuyGS54EFVMUdhaP4htD3F*

page 66: *youtube.com/watch?time_continue=25&v=yTGSy-79eHc*

page 72: *youtube.com/watch?v=gn4nRCC9TwQ*

page 74: *eyes.nasa.gov/curiosity*

RESOURCES

QR CODE GLOSSARY (CONTINUED)

page 75: *nasa.gov/audience/foreducators/robotics/home/index.html*

page 75: *solarsystem.nasa.gov*

page 75: *nasa.gov/mission_pages/station/main/index.html*

page 77: *roboticstomorrow.com/article/2015/12/ the-new-family-member-a-robotic-caregiver/7312*

page 79: *shelleygodwinarchive.org/contents/frankenstein*

page 79: *rc.umd.edu/editions/frankenstein*

page 80: *librivox.org/rur-rossums-universal-robots-by-karel-capek*

page 82: *youtube.com/watch?v=AWJJnQybZlk*

page 83: *tcm.com/mediaroom/video/1102413/ Day-The-Earth-Stood-Still-The-Original-Trailer-.html*

page 85: *tcm.com/mediaroom/video/474156/ 2001-A-Space-Odyssey-Movie-Clip-HAL-9000.html*

page 88: *tcm.com/mediaroom/video/188651/Terminator-The-Original-Trailer-.html*

page 101: *theguardian.com/technology/2018/mar/19/ uber-self-driving-car-kills-woman-arizona-tempe*

ESSENTIAL QUESTIONS

Introduction: Is there a difference between acting intelligent and being intelligent?

Chapter 1: How did the definition of AI change during the twentieth century?

Chapter 2: How has AI exploded in the twenty-first century?

Chapter 3: How might AI improve human lives in the future?

Chapter 4: What might today's world be like without the influence of AI?

Chapter 5: How do science fiction movies and books reflect our attitudes toward robots and AI in the real world?

Chapter 6: Will AIs take over the world like they sometimes do in science fiction books and movies?

INDEX

A

activities
  Build a Model of a Neuron, 34
  Can an AI Do Your Dream Job?, 110
  Code on Paper, 24–25
  Compare and Contrast, 96
  Crafting the Uncanny Valley, 56
  Debate the Great AI Debate, 109
  Design a Caregiver or Companion
    Robot, 77
  Design a Rescue Robot, 74
  Design a Space Robot, 75
  Detecting Patterns, 39
  Explore Scratch! Make a Maze Game,
    23
  Exploring the Uncanny Valley, 55
  Learn to Play Go, 40
  Make a Bugbot, 60–61
  Make a Neural Network, 38
  Make a Robot, 58–59
  Meme the Future!, 57
  Neurons Firing!, 35
  Perceptron, 36–37
  Self-Driving Cars Today, 62
  Spot an Algorithm in the Wild, 76
  Take a Turing Test, 9
  Write Your Own Laws of Robotics, 94
  Write Your Own Short Story or Poem
    About AIs or Robots, 95
Alexa, v, 7, 26, 27–29
algorithms, 6, 17, 21, 33, 53, 76, 100
AlphaGo, v, 6, 26, 30–31, 40
Antikythera mechanism, 11–12
artificial intelligence (AI)
  benefits of. *See* benefits of artificial
    intelligence
  current state of, v, 6–7, 26–40
  debate around, 97–110
  definition and description of, 1–2
  early, iv–v, 10–25
  future of, 7, 41–62
  humans vs., 2–6. *See also* humans
  research areas for, 7, 16, 101. *See also*
    DARPA challenge
  robots. *See* robots
  science fiction with, iv, 78–96
  strong vs. weak, 6, 19
  terminology for, iv, 16

Asimov, Isaac, iv, 82, 83, 94

B

Babbage, Charles, 12–13
banking AI uses, 12–13, 19–20
benefits of artificial intelligence. *See also*
  other specific uses
  data management, 7, 21, 31, 33, 71, 99,
    106, 108
  debate about, 97–110
  household uses, v, 46, 69
  human connections, 72–73
  medical uses, 7, 18, 19, 26, 31, 44, 46,
    68–71 . *See also* elder care robots
  overview of, 63
  safety uses, 43, 64–67, 74–75
bionics, 69
Blade Runner, 89
Bostrom, Nick, 102–103

C

C-3PO, iv, 86, 87
checkers, 17, 20
chess, iv, 2–5, 11, 15, 17
Colossus, 14
creative artificial intelligence, 53–54,
  58–59
current artificial intelligence
  AI assistants, v, 7, 26, 27–29, 33
  AlphaGo, 6, 26, 30–31, 40
  games, 6–7, 26, 30–31, 32, 33, 40
  machine learning, 6, 27, 28, 31, 40
  medical AI uses, 7, 26, 31
  neural networks, 31, 33, 34–39
  overview of, v, 6–7, 26
  police AI uses, 26, 32–33
  speech and language processing, 7, 27,
    33
CyberKnife, 68
cyberpunk, 89

D

DARPA challenge, v, 43, 46, 47, 64, 65, 66, 74
Data, Lt. Commander, 91
data management, 7, 21, 31, 33, 71, 99, 106, 108
da Vinci Surgical System, 68
The Day the Earth Stood Still, 83–84, 93
debate, artificial intelligence, 97–110
Deep Blue, iv, 2–5, 32
DeepMind, 30, 31, 72, 98, 99
Difference Engine, 12, 13
Doctor Who, 88
Douglas, Alexander, 24

E

early artificial intelligence
  AI spring/growth, 19–20
  AI winter/slow-down, iv, 18–19
  chatting/talking, 17–18, 20
  first computers, 12–14
  games, 15, 17, 24–25
  machine learning, 17, 20–22
  overview of, iv–v, 10–11
  pre-computers, 11–12
  terminology, 16
  Turing, Turing Machine, Turing Test, iv, 13, 14–15, 16, 20
elder care robots, 44, 46, 73, 77
ELIZA, iv, 18, 19
Ellie, 72
ElliQ, 46
essential questions, 8, 22, 33, 54, 73, 93, 108
exoskeletons, 70

F

Frankenstein (Shelley), 79
future artificial intelligence
  creative AI, 53–54, 58–59
  imagining, 7, 41
  robots, 42–46, 55–56, 58–61
  self-driving cars, 46, 47–53, 62
fuzzy logic, 17, 20

G

games
  checkers, 17, 20
  chess, iv, 2–5, 11, 15, 17
  current AI playing, 6–7, 26, 30–31, 32, 33, 40
  early AI playing, 15, 17, 24–25
  Go/AlphaGo, v, 6, 26, 30–31, 40
  Jeopardy!, v, 7, 32
  tic-tac-toe, 17, 24–25
  video games, 24
GiraffPlus, 46
Go, v, 6, 30–31, 40
Google
  DeepMind, 30, 31, 72, 98, 99
  Google Assistant, 26, 27–29
  Magenta Project, 54
  neural network development, 106
  self-driving car development, 47–48, 51, 53, 67
Gort, 83–84

H

HAL 9000, 85–86
humans
  elder care robots for, 44, 46, 73, 77
  intelligence of, 2
  labor issues among, 81, 103–108
  machine vs., 2–6. *See also* artificial intelligence
  medical AI for, 7, 18, 19, 26, 31, 44, 46, 68–71
  neural networks, 34–35
  self-driving car interface with, 48, 52, 101
  social robots connecting with, 7, 42–46, 72–73, 77
  speech and language from, 7, 20, 26, 27–29, 33

I

I, Robot (Asimov), 83, 93
IBM
  AI research, 16
  checkers program, 17
  Deep Blue, 2–5, 32
  Watson, v, 26, 31–32, 53, 71, 72
internet, 20, 21, 91
Internet of Things (IoT), 29

J

Jeopardy!, v, 7, 32
jobs/labor issues, 81, 103–108

K

Kasparov, Garry, iv, 2–5

L

language. *See* programming languages;
  speech and language
lawn mowers, robotic, 69
lidar, 49–50, 51
Lovelace, Ada, 13

M

machine learning
  current AI and, 6, 27, 28, 31, 40
  debate about, 99, 100, 106
  early AI and, 17, 20–22
  future AI and, 54
The Matrix, 90–91, 93
McCarthy, John, iv, 16
medical AI uses, 7, 18, 19, 26, 31, 44, 46,
  68–71. *See also* elder care robots
Metropolis, 81–82, 93
military AI uses, 13, 14, 43, 86, 101
Musk, Elon, 97–99, 102

N

NAO, 44–45
natural language processing, iv, 7, 27, 33
neural networks, 20–22, 31, 33, 34–39,
  106
Neuromancer (Gibson), 89–90

O

OpenAI, 99, 101
Oz of Ozma (Baum), 80

P

paper clip scenario, 102–103
Paro, 44
patterns/pattern matching, 14, 18, 39
Pepper, 7, 44
police AI uses, 26, 32–33, 71
privacy issues, 108
programming languages, iv, 16, 17–18, 23

R

R2-D2, iv, 86, 87
radar, 49–50
Robby the Robot, 81
Robear, 46
RoboBee, 60
robots
  early, 12
  future, 42–46, 55–56, 58–61
  household uses, v, 46, 69
  Laws of Robotics, iv, 82, 83, 94
  medical uses, 44, 46, 68, 70 (*see also*
    elder care robots)
  safety uses, 43, 64–67, 74, 75
  science fiction with, 79–96
  social, 7, 42–46, 72–73, 77
Rossum's Universal Robots (Čapek), 80,
  81–82

INDEX

S

safety uses and concerns, v, 43, 53, 64–67, 74–75, 101
Samuel, Arthur, 17, 20
science fiction artificial intelligence
  overview of, 78
  ancient to 19th century, 79–80
  early 20th century, 80–82
  mid-20th century, 83–84
  1960s and 1970s, iv, 85–88
  late 20th century, 88–91
  early 21st century, 91–93
search-and-rescue robots, 64, 65, 74
self-driving cars, v, 7, 46, 47–53, 62, 66–67, 101
singularity, 98, 99, 102
Siri, v, 7, 26, 27–29
Sophia, 42
SoundNet, 33
space exploration, v, 64–65, 66, 74, 75
speech and language, iv, 7, 17–18, 20, 26, 27–29, 33
Star Trek: The Next Generation, 91
Star Wars, iv, 86, 87, 93
The Steam Man of the Prairies (Ellis), 80

T

The Terminator, 88, 93
Tesla, 48, 49, 51, 67
tic-tac-toe, 17, 24–25
Tik-Tok, 80
Turing, Alan/Turing test/Turing Machine, iv, v, 9, 13, 14–15, 16, 20
2001: A Space Odyssey, iv, 85–86, 93

U

Uber, 48, 51, 53
uncanny valley, 43, 55–56

V

vacuum cleaners, robotic, v, 46, 69
Valkyrie, 65, 66, 74, 75

W

Wall-E, 92, 93
WarGames, 86, 93
Watson, v, 26, 31–32, 53, 71, 72
Westworld, 86–87, 93

Z

Z3 computer, 14
Zuckerberg, Mark, 97, 99–100
Zuse, Konrad, 14